UNSINKABLE

A YOUNG WOMAN'S COURAGEOUS BATTLE
ON THE HIGH SEAS

Abby Sunderland
and Lynn Vincent

THOMAS NELSON
Since 1798

NASHVILLE   DALLAS   MEXICO CITY   RIO DE JANEIRO

Published in Nashville, Tennessee, by Thomas Nelson. Thomas Nelson is a registered trademark of Thomas Nelson, Inc.

Author is represented by the literary agency of Alive Communications, Inc., 7680 Goddard Street, Suite 200, Colorado Springs, CO, 80920.

Thomas Nelson, Inc., titles may be purchased in bulk for educational, business, fund-raising, or sales promotional use. For information, please e-mail SpecialMarkets@ ThomasNelson.com.

Unless otherwise noted, Scripture quotations are taken from THE NEW KING JAMES VERSION. © 1982 by Thomas Nelson, Inc. Used by permission. All rights reserved.

Library of Congress Cataloging-in-Publication Data

Sunderland, Abby, 1993-
  Unsinkable : a young woman's courageous battle on the high seas / Abby Sunderland and Lynn Vincent.
      p. cm.
  Includes bibliographical references and index.
  ISBN 978-1-4002-0308-6 (alk. paper)
  1. Sunderland, Abby, 1993- 2. Women sailors--United States--Biography. 3. Women adventurers--United States--Biography. 4. Voyages around the world. 5. Single-handed sailing. I. Vincent, Lynn. II. Title.
  GV810.92.S86A3 2011
  797.1092--dc22
  [B]

                                        2011000486

Printed in the United States of America
11 12 13 14 15 QGF 6 5 4 3 2 1

To Mom, for all your hard work behind the scenes.
You really did so much for me and my trip.

To Dad, for supporting my decision and believing
in me and my dream.

Thank you both for your love and encouragement.

CONTENTS

If I take the wings of the morning,
And dwell in the uttermost parts of the sea,
Even there Your hand shall lead me,
And Your right hand shall hold me.

—PSALM 139:9–10

AUTHORS' NOTE

Throughout the book, there are three icons. One represents Abby's voice ◣. Another represents the narrator's voice ⚓. The third represents those who took part in the rescue efforts to save Abby in the Indian Ocean ✚. A change in icon indicates a change in speaker or location.

For a map of Abby's route, see page 202. For an illustration of Abby's boat, *Wild Eyes*, see page 204.

THE INDIAN OCEAN

 There are a number of places on marine charts where even the most weathered sailors point and say, *"Right there, nothing can go wrong. Everything has to go right."* One place is the turbulent passage south of Cape Horn. Another is the dead center of the Indian Ocean.

Eclipsed in size only by the Pacific and Atlantic, the Indian Ocean covers 14 percent of the earth's surface—twenty-seven million square miles. Its waters are bounded on the north by the wide skirt of Southeast Asia, including India, and on the west by the African continent. To the east, the Indian churns ashore in Australia and Indochina. To the south, only Antarctica hems it in. Its vast waters are jeweled with exotic island nations like Madagascar, an eighteenth-century haven for pirates, and the Maldives, whose powder blue waters are home to twenty-six different kinds of sharks.

At turns beautiful and deadly, the Indian Ocean can charm sailors with fair winds and crisp, sunny days topside—or challenge them to a lightning-charged duel, man against sea. Even less than a hundred years ago, having your boat become disabled in the middle of the Indian's immense rolling reaches was as good as a death sentence. A captain could only hope his rum didn't run out before his life did.

Because of modern technology, the odds are better today, but not much. The center of the Indian Ocean is two thousand miles from any search-and-rescue operation of significant size. That means any search plane that could fly low enough to spot a foundering sailboat would not have the fuel capacity to reach it.

- -

COMMANDERS' WEATHER
(MARINE WEATHER SERVICE)

FORECAST: JUNE 9, 2010

1230 UTC (GREENWICH MEAN TIME):

LOOK OUT FOR AN INCREASING NW TO N WIND BY 15 UTC WED, AND THEN WILL BE A VERY ROUGH PERIOD MAINLY BETWEEN 21 UTC WED TO ABOUT 06 OR 09 UTC THU, AS THIS NEXT STORM SYSTEM APPROACHES . . .

AS TROUGH PUSHES THRU, THERE WILL BE SOME SQUALLS, W/GUSTS UP TO 50-60 KTS POSSIBLE BY 21 UTC TODAY. BEHIND THIS TROUGH, WIND SHIFTS INTO NW, AND WILL BE QUITE STRONG FROM NW AHEAD OF COLD FRONT THRU ABOUT 0600-0900 UTC.

THIS NW WIND MAY BE SUSTAINED AT 35-50 KTS, AND COULD BE SQUALLS TO 60 KTS OVERALL.

WILL BE ABOUT A 9-12 HR PERIOD OF ROUGHEST CONDITIONS.

- -

The storms were amazing—sometimes even fun. *Wild Eyes* was built for speed and I was flying down walls of water twenty and thirty feet high. As a sailor, you dream of seeing waves like that, rolling mountains of water that look like they're covered in dark gray silk. During the day, vast dark clouds hung low over the water. Sometimes the sun shined through in places. At night, the weather often cleared and I clipped myself in up on deck, racing along the swells under stars so big and bright they lit up the night like extra moons.

But in the second week of June, storms roared in one after another—bashing *Wild Eyes*, my open 40 boat, shredding her sails, knocking out my gear. There was very little time between blows to patch up the damage. One day a screaming wind tore my genoa, the big sail on the front of the boat. What a pain! You have to thread the sail up the furler and it flogs all over the place while you're doing it, gets jammed, then sticks like a zipper. When that happens, you have to run it back down the furler and start over. In twenty-knot winds, it took a whole day to run up a new genoa. Another day the sail ties on my mainsail came loose and I had to climb all over the boom like a monkey trying to secure it again. The storm whipped the 120-pound Kevlar sail back and forth like it was as flimsy as a bed sheet.

Repairing my sails was job number one. Without them, *Wild Eyes* was helpless. But fixing sails ate up the short lulls between storms, leaving the rest of the damage—and the work—to pile up. I was already running on secondary autopilot and it wasn't working all that well. I had fixed a leak under the throttle, but the leak popped loose again, pouring seawater back into the compartment. The heater was broken, so I couldn't get dry between blows, and I couldn't shake off the numbing cold. Meanwhile, as I tried to do repairs, the storms tossed me back and forth across the tiny cabin so much that I began to feel like a giant pinball.

I tried to keep the mind-set: *Don't get overwhelmed. Do one thing at a time. That's all you can do.*

The open ocean often takes you past your physical limits and when it does, sailing becomes a mental game. When fear starts to flicker in your brain, you have to stop it quickly before it turns into something bad. As soon as you let your thoughts start racing down the road of what *could* happen, what *might* happen, fear can snatch you up and run away with you. Nothing good comes from that. Fear causes hesitation instead of decisive action. At sea, you have to think fast, be ready at any moment to make big decisions. You can't waste time being scared. You can't risk it.

But I would learn that some challenges are greater than others. And fear can tear its way into your heart no matter how tough you think you are.

On June 10, the worst storm in the series swept across the middle of the Indian Ocean, and *Wild Eyes* was directly in its path. Four times during the day, massive waves and winds knocked my boat completely down, putting my mast in the water. I was below and if I wasn't strapped in, the force lifted me from wherever I was in the cabin and threw me against the wall. And every time, the autopilot went into standby mode. Once *Wild Eyes* started to right herself, I had to race topside, jump in the cockpit, and grab the tiller to hand steer the boat back on course.

Each time I opened the companionway door, *Wild Eyes* was heeled way over toward the heaving sea. Outside the wind was screaming. Waves sloshed across my head, smashing into my face, sucking my breath away. I had to clip my harness to a railing then rise up through the companionway. The boat's deck had become a high wall on my right, forcing me to find footing along the skinny inside wall of the cockpit, which was now slightly submerged. I stepped out. The boat dipped wildly and saltwater whipped across my face, spraying the vertical deck as I picked my way along the cockpit wall. I tried not to think about the fact that my feet were wading on the edge of nowhere, that the nearest land was Kerguelen Island, a little rock seven hundred miles south. But it was a hard fact that wouldn't go away. Fear pecked at me, and I tried to swat it away by moving, moving, moving. Get to the cockpit. Grab the tiller. Steer the boat.

The fourth knockdown was the worst. Even before I opened the hatch, I knew my mast was well in the water—a potential disaster. Heart pounding, I listened as the howling wind banged the rigging against the mast, and waited.

How far will it go? Will the weight of the mast, of the water in the tiny bit of staysail, keep pulling me over? Will I roll?

No!

I felt *Wild Eyes* rally against the sea—again!—and begin to right herself.

Relief surged through me. *I* love *this boat!*

But it wasn't all good news. The Indian Ocean had ripped my radar right off the carbon-fiber mast and swallowed it whole. The radar had been secured to the mast with four huge steel bolts. The sea had pulled the gear off as easily as the pop-top on a tuna can, and it reminded me who was boss. Still, the mast was upright again and I had all my sails. *Wild Eyes'* resilience inspired me.

Okay, that was the worst of it, I thought. *I'll just hang on until things calm down.*

And they did. Early that evening, I stood on the deck in the stiff wind and looked out at the rolling sea. The gray daylight had melted away and it was full dark. The moon rose behind the clouds and found patches to shine through, like a flashlight from God. The waves were still huge, but they seemed less angry, the swells glinting silver in the moonlight. Just before dark, I had pulled the staysail all the way out to take advantage of the easier winds. Now I stood still, hand on the rigging, and turned my face into the freezing salt spray. I was already exhausted from pulling all-nighters to patch up my boat. Physically, I was getting pretty worn down. Emotionally, too. For now the worst was over, but Commanders' Weather had forecast another big storm ahead. I needed to start pulling *Wild Eyes* back together. I went below to prioritize the workload.

Even with the outer hatch closed, I could still hear the wind roaring through the rigging and sails, and the bass sound of the boat rushing through the water. Pitched by the waves, the cabin rocked gunwale to gunwale. To get around and inspect the damage, I had to hang on tight to the series of handrails bolted to the inside bulkheads. The cabin light was dim and yellow. Handing my way to the chart desk, I checked my battery gauge. I was down to 12.1 volts, not enough to power the auto-pilots through the night. Time to run the engines, charge it up a little.

The engine box was in the middle of the cabin, near my bed, which was a narrow cot that folded down from the wall just below a set of wall-mounted gauges and a calendar with kittens on it, my substitute for having a real boat cat. Most people who want a four-legged ship-mate choose a cat, and I'd always wanted a cat to go sailing with. I had considered getting one during my stop in Cape Town, but I figured the freezing, damp conditions wouldn't be fair to the cat, so I settled for the calendar instead.

I turned, bent to the engine box, and pressed the starter switch. All I heard was a click.

I tried it again. Click.

Again. Click.

Great. It must've gotten wet during one of the knockdowns.

Mentally, I ticked through my options. I was pretty good with engine work, but if I diagnosed the problem wrong and didn't get it running soon, the autopilot would go belly up. I knew I was too exhausted and the conditions too rough to hand steer through the night, and with no autopilot that would be the only way I could stay on course. Plus, if my battery got too low, I'd have no chart plotter, no wind gauges, no radio, not even lights. I thought the best idea was to call my support team for some troubleshooting help. That was my best chance for getting it right the first time.

At this longitude, it was eleven hours earlier in California, which put the time there at 4:00 in the morning. I felt terrible. I knew Mom was very pregnant and I hated the thought of her having to roll (literally) out of bed at that hour. I picked up the Iridium phone and switched it on. Jeff Casher was my all-purpose technical guy, and a great troubleshooter.

Sorry, Jeff, you're "it," I thought, and started dialing.

 In Thousand Oaks, Marianne Sunderland's cell phone rang in the dark bedroom, and she came awake instantly. She'd had teenagers at sea for two years running and was used to it. In the unified dance of thought and action peculiar to mothers, she plucked the phone off her nightstand, recognized Abby's sat-phone number, noted the time, and went on mild alert.

Marianne answered the phone: "Abby?"

The call dropped immediately.

Beside Marianne, Laurence Sunderland stirred. "What is it?"

"Abby, but the call dropped."

"A bit early for her call, eh?" Laurence ran his hands down his face, across the dark stubble on his jaws and chin.

"That's what I was thinking. I was going to call Jeff."

"Right. Let's see if he's online."

Marianne and Laurence got out of bed and walked the few steps to the small alcove off their bedroom that they'd converted to an office. Each had a desk set up in there, along with bookcases and a couple of sturdy, metal filing cabinets. The space overflowed with paperwork, maps, and nautical charts, but the Sunderlands had a crack organizing system. Laurence didn't fancy filing things, but he couldn't work unless his desk was clear. So he transferred his paper piles to Marianne's desk, where she kept track of both their piles in the way an archeologist keeps track of a particularly complicated dig. It worked for them.

With Laurence looking on over her shoulder, Marianne cued up Skype, an online messaging and video-conferencing system. Jeff Casher and his wife, Gail, had spent eight years circumnavigating the globe. Jeff was also an electronics and computer expert who worked with high profile clients including eBay and AT&T. He was very much in demand, so if he was awake, he would be online.

Marianne messaged him: "Hi, Jeff. Abby called, but the call dropped. Are you up?"

An answer appeared on Marianne's monitor: "Yeah, I'm talking to her right now. She can't start her engine. I'll set up the bridge and patch you guys in."

The "bridge" was what Jeff called a telephone communications system that allowed several people to participate in a conference call. The Sunderlands had found it invaluable for unraveling the knotty technical problems that had arisen during Abby's "campaign," as Laurence called it, using the proper British term for a sailing expedition.

When the autopilots were on the blink, or the heater down, or the water maker on the fritz (or, or, or . . .), the team confabbed on the bridge. Between Laurence, a career shipwright and experienced boat captain; Scott Lurie, an expert marine electrician and mechanic; and Jeff, they'd been able to troubleshoot and conquer potentially voyage-ending problems.

The Sunderlands believed God had blessed them with a great team to support Abby's solo attempt. They had grown especially close to Jeff and Scott, who were as different on the outside as the Odd Couple—with Jeff (buttoned-down and mannered) as Felix Unger, and Scott (shaggy and unpressed) as Oscar Madison. But they were so much alike in their technical acumen, their ability to turn a problem every which way until it was solved, that they sometimes spoke each other's thoughts aloud. Someone once commented that the two men were like sorority sisters whose cycles had lined up after living in the same dorm for a while. Jeff and Scott, who already loved poking fun at each other, thought that was hysterically funny and started calling each other "Sister."

Now Jeff's voice came through the speakerphone. "Marianne? Laurence? I woke up Sister Scott. He's on."

"G'day, Scott," Laurence said cheerily. "How's the morning treating you?"

"It ain't morning til it's light," Scott said with a smile in his voice. "This ain't it."

"Listen," Jeff said. "I've talked with Abby a couple of times. The calls keep dropping, but the short version is that she's had a pretty rough day, got knocked down a couple of times. Her engine won't start and she's frustrated."

Just then, Abby joined the call.

"Hi, Dad." Abby's voice sounded high and small. Tired. Worry nipped at Marianne because she knew her daughter was a tough nut to crack.

"Hey, Ab," Laurence said. "What's going on?"

"My engine won't start."

"Alright, tell me what you've done so far."

The call dropped.

"Blast," Laurence said mildly. He and Marianne stared at the weather and marine chart software on their computer screen, its faint glow lighting the office. Their modest, one-story home spread quietly around them, six children sleeping in other rooms.

Abby called right back and didn't waste time. "The only thing I've done is recycle the starter switch. My batteries are low and it's already dark. I knew I needed to get it fixed fast, so I called."

"Well, you've probably got water in the engine from knockdowns—" Laurence started to say.

The call dropped.

"She sounds exhausted," Marianne said. Scott and Jeff made general sounds of agreement.

Abby popped up on the bridge again and Laurence got right to it: "What you need to do, Ab, is flip the compression lock lever." That would hold the exhaust valves open and enable the engine to turn over, and pump out the seawater. "Remember, Scott and I showed you how to do that?"

"Yes . . ." Abby said. Muffled clicks on the other end, then an engine sound against a background of howling clatter. Laurence recognized the sound. *Wild Eyes'* rigging was banging against the mast in a wicked wind. In all of Abby's calls home, he'd never heard that before. Troubling.

But then his daughter came on the line again, sounding relieved. "It started. It's working."

"What are your conditions, Abby?" It was Jeff.

"Winds about thirty-five knots."

"What are the seas?"

"Twenty to thirty feet."

"Wow," Marianne said.

Abby laughed. "That's nothing compared to what I had before. This is easy!"

The call dropped.

CHAPTER 1

ISLA GUADALUPE

BAJA, CALIFORNIA, MEXICO
2001

 "Look, Dad! A panga!" Abby called to Laurence as they made their approach to Isla Guadalupe off the western coast of Baja, California, the northernmost state in Mexico. The island was home to fewer than fifteen people, mostly abalone and lobster fishermen. It would be the Sunderlands' first port of call on what had long been a family dream: cruising the Mexican coast in their own boat.

Dusk was falling softly as *Amazing Grace*, the Sunderlands' Aleutian 51, slipped quietly past Isla Guadalupe's southern end into majestic Melpomene Cove. Laurence and Marianne, along with Zac, then 10; Abby, 8; Toby, 4; and Jessica, 3, gathered at the bow and peered up in awe. To port, orange-tinted cliffs towered seven hundred feet, sheltering the cove from the sea; to starboard, sheer rock faces soared skyward. Below, even in the gloaming light, Laurence could see fifty feet down through the green water straight to the ocean floor.

Now the panga Abby had spotted motored closer. It was the kind of long, narrow skiff that forms the backbone of the Mexican fishing industry, and Laurence could see a man standing astride the beam, waving both arms like a signalman.

"*Hola, senor!*" the man called. "*Cerveza para langosta? Cerveza para langosta?*"

Laurence flashed Marianne a puzzled look. Everybody from Southern California knows that *cerveza* means beer. But what in the world was *langosta*? As the panga drew near, the Sunderlands saw the answer: the man was a lobster fisherman and his day's catch was scuttling around in the bottom of his boat. Several dozen Pacific lobsters, rosy brown in color, crawled on top of one another like giant ants in a colony.

"Wow," Zac said. "*Look* at all those!" Abby, Jessica, and Toby peered down into the panga, fascinated.

"Ah, *langosta!*" Laurence said. "Lobster! *Si, senor!*" Mentally searching through his limited Spanish vocabulary, he came up with a number. "We'll take four . . . *cuarenta!*"

The man's weathered brown face cracked into a wide grin. "*Cuarenta! Muy bien!*"

"No, *espera! Espera!*" Marianne called to the man, using the Spanish word for *wait*. Then to Laurence: "Um, I think *cuarenta* means forty."

"No, wait, wait!" Laurence cried to the fisherman, waving his arms. "*Espera! Espera!*"

But the fisherman had already begun pitching lobsters up onto *Amazing Grace*, where they scuttled across the deck like desperados in a prison break. The Sunderland kids broke into fits of giggles, bending over the new passengers to follow their progress and dancing back and forth to keep their toes out of claw reach.

Between the Sunderlands' broken Spanish and the fisherman's scant English, the Sunderlands wound up with a dozen fresh lobsters for the price of a twelve-pack of beer that someone had given them back on Catalina Island before they set sail.

Laurence gathered the lobsters in a bucket and assembled the kids in the cockpit where they watched wide-eyed as he expertly twisted off the crustaceans' heads and chucked them over the side. A pot of boiling water later, along with garlic butter for dipping, the Sunderlands enjoyed the first of three years of seaborne feasts.

 In 2001, after three attempts, broken autopilots, and an IRS audit, the Sunderlands set sail on the cruise of a lifetime. Not a cruise where you book passage on a big liner, lounge in deck chairs, and gamble in the ship's casino, but cruis*ing*, where you sail your own boat from port to port and linger in the ones you like.

Laurence had just finished two seasons working as harbor patrolman in the Emerald Bay area of Santa Catalina Island. Harbor patrolmen are responsible for watching over the bay in which they are stationed. They take radio calls from boats coming into the bay and assign them moorings and also assist boats in trouble in their area.

Laurence brought to the job a lifetime of experience. Born in England in a town called New Milton, he had grown up in what he calls a "golden triangle" of sailing. New Milton is near the coastal town of Lymington, which is directly across the solent from the Isle of Wight, the original site of the America's Cup race. Directly east of Lymington is Portsmouth, the site of several major yacht races, such as the Fastnet and the Whitbread.

The son of a piano tuner who also ran a commercial fishing business, Laurence had his first boat before his first bicycle. It was a dinghy that he kept shipshape. From the age of about ten, Laurence and his friends would row the dinghy up the channels off the Lymington River near their home, beach it on the sedge banks, and hunt for seagull eggs. Then they'd build a fire and fry up the eggs for breakfast. While sailing with his father, Laurence developed a passion for the sea. At age sixteen, he finished secondary school—the American equivalent of high school—but decided against college. An outdoorsman all his life, he hated sitting in a classroom, so he decided to turn his passion into an occupation and began an apprenticeship as a boat builder. From master tradesmen, he learned every aspect of the field: sheet metal, fiberglassing, electronics, plumbing, welding, and both construction and finish carpentry.

By the time he was nineteen, though, a newly enacted luxury tax had begun to cripple the British boating industry. So, Laurence moved to Australia, where he worked in commercial carpentry and picked up a couple of boat-building gigs. He also became involved in music, with a band called Xyphoid, as manager, songwriter, and lead singer. The band enjoyed moderate success in Australia, so in 1990, they set out to conquer the music capitals of the world, including Los Angeles.

That's where Laurence encountered the most beautiful woman he had ever seen. He had just cut some recordings at an L.A. studio and come away with an awful headache. While in Australia, he had discovered that surfing was great medicine, so he drove over to Venice Beach. Just as he tossed his towel on the beach and parked his surfboard in the sand, Laurence saw a slim, fit young woman in her early twenties sitting near the water's edge. She seemed to be keeping an eye on four teenage boys who were wading in the whitewater.

Wearing shorts and a T-shirt, the woman had long, light brown hair with hints of strawberry. Instantly smitten, Laurence angled for an opening. "You look too young to have such old children," was what he finally came up with.

The woman smiled. "Oh, these aren't my kids. I'm working."

She introduced herself as Marianne. A recent graduate of Cal State Northridge, she had a degree in psychology. The kids were from a group home for teens from troubled families, Marianne explained. She was their counselor.

For her part, Marianne was charmed by the blond, blue-eyed surfer with the Aussie accent. They agreed to meet later for a date, but neither had a pen and paper to exchange contact information. Laurence was so determined to see Marianne again that he used his car key to carve her phone number right into the leather of one of his high-top tennis shoes.

While Xyphoid showed promise in Australia and Los Angeles, the band eventually folded. So Laurence returned to his trade, opening Sunderland Yacht Management in 1990. He married Marianne the following year.

Later, as their family grew, so did Laurence's dream of family cruising. In 1998, when the opportunity arose for Laurence to work as a harbor patrolman at Catalina Island, the Sunderlands felt it would be an ideal way to test both their boat and their family for life at sea.

At Emerald Bay they lived on a mooring with no dock or shore power, no grocery store, and no laundromat. The arrangement gave them the opportunity to test the Aleutian's ability to generate solar, wind, and diesel power—and test the Sunderlands' ability to conserve power. The family learned to provision—or buy supplies—for two and three weeks at a time. They made their own water with an onboard desalinator.

The kids loved Emerald Bay. Most days, Marianne would row to the island and take them to the beach. Sometimes Zac and Abby would swim to shore or row Zac's little sailing dinghy over on their own. All the kids learned to snorkel, fish, and kayak.

But since Laurence's harbor patrol duties lasted year-round, the children also had academic learning to do. A little more than twenty miles off the coast of Los Angeles, Santa Catalina's rich history gave Marianne material for interesting homeschool lessons. Originally, the island was home to a native tribe called the Pimu. Spanish explorer Juan Cabrillo was the first European to walk the island's shores in 1542. He christened it San Salvador. Another explorer, Sebastian Vizcaino, rediscovered the island in 1602 and named it Santa Catalina after the Catholic saint, Catherine.

The next three centuries drew a parade of colorful visitors—from Yankee smugglers to the Aleut tribe of what was then part of Russia but is now Alaska. Pirates also favored Santa Catalina because they could hide out in its secluded coves. Laurence Sunderland preferred to charm his kids with pirate stories, while Marianne created hands-on science lessons about the island's wildlife, like deer mice and island fox, and history lessons about the Aleutians, who had come to the island and hunted the otters to extinction.

Living on the boat during Laurence's harbormaster years was the family's preparation for a real family cruise that they hoped might end with them sailing into Laurence's home port of Lymington. Before undertaking a long voyage, it was important to the Sunderlands to make sure the family could live on the boat and be happy and functional. In Laurence's mind, there would be nothing worse than taking your wife and kids cruising if they were going to suffer the whole time or be unable to adjust to life at sea. He wanted the cruise to be something that was uplifting and exciting, something that would draw his family close together. Both Laurence and Marianne also wanted their kids to develop responsibility, to see other cultures, and to experience the world instead of watching it on TV.

The most important part of the equation was safety. Laurence made sure the kids understood being at sea was anything but a lark. The cruising life can be quite mundane for long periods of time, but when things go wrong, they can go wrong quickly.

"Out there, if you're forgetful or disobedient, you don't get a time-out," he explained without theatrics. "If you don't tie down your surfboard, you lose your surfboard. If you don't tie up your dinghy, you lose your dinghy. If you slip and fall and you're not tethered, and the boat is moving and no one sees you, you could fall overboard and be gone."

On October 21, after a last push to prepare their vessel, the fifty-one-foot Aleutian cutter-rigged sailboat *Amazing Grace*, the Sunderlands—Captain Laurence, First Mate Marianne, and Able Seamen Zac, Abby, Toby, and Jessie—set sail for Mexico.

Laurence and Marianne were both amazed at how their children handled the passages between ports. They entertained themselves by building forts, reading books, or pretending to be Indians, and never seemed bored. At only two and a half, Jessica was the most sure-footed, having learned to walk while living aboard a boat. (As a comical result, on land Jessica rarely walked in a straight line.) Zac and Abby were both cheerful, eager to help with sails and lines and galley chores. But poor Toby never quite got over his seasickness. The Sunderlands watched him closely, hoping that he would rebound after a day or two at sea like the other kids.

One key element of the cruising life was shared responsibilities. Grocery shopping, for example, was an errand that required all hands on deck. Marianne, Laurence, and the four kids would pile into the dinghy, everyone wearing a backpack. From anchorage in the bay of Tenacatita, for example, Laurence would motor the dinghy to shore and from there the family clambered out and walked to the bus stop where they caught a jalopy bus to town. From Tenacatita, the bus rumbled through the dusty village of La Manzanilla and on to Melaque, a center for local commerce. *Las tiendas*, the stores, were squat stucco buildings with the proprietors' names hand-painted on the chipped plaster walls. Inside, Marianne and the kids dug scoops into oak barrels filled with *arroz, frijoles*, and *azúcar* (rice, beans, and sugar) and filled plastic Hefty bags with staple supplies.

Marianne showed Abby and Zac how to select the best papayas and bananas, and all four kids loved the treat of raw sugar cane, which they could peel and chew until it produced a light sweetness.

Once, in Melaque, a four-year-old Mexican girl, keeping her mama company in one of the *tiendas*, introduced Abby to the fuzzy yellow chick she was playing with. Abby fell in love and spent that whole night making a list of possible names for the pet chicken she was suddenly bound and determined to get. (Back in America, a couple of years later, she did get one: a free-range chicken hand-raised by a neighbor who had taught the bird to sit next to humans and nibble grain out of their hands.)

After all the shopping, the last stop was the *tortilleria*, where a chattering klatch of short, round Mexican ladies patted cornmeal mash into flat discs and tossed them onto a griddle where they transformed into soft, warm, chewy delights. Marianne would buy a dozen tortillas for seven *pesos*, and she and the kids would eat them all on the bus ride back to the dinghy. It was the kind of little ritual that lifelong memories are made of.

While the family could buy enough staples to last awhile, fresh food ran out quickly. Luckily, from Tenacatita they could motor their dinghy up a saltwater stream under a canopy of mangroves to an enchanting bay called the Aquarium because of its abundance of bright tropical fish. There were no hotels or businesses to speak of there, only a couple of palapas sheltering tiny outdoor restaurants. Once a week, a man driving a produce truck would rumble in to supply the restaurants. The cruisers anchored at Tenacatita knew this and would motor through the mangroves to buy his goods.

For the Sunderlands, the dinghy ride was always long and a bit wild, as they buzzed slowly under low-hanging mangroves flitting with blue-footed boobies and tiny, bright finches. Every now and then, the kids would spot a crocodile dozing on a bank-side boulder. But the crocs seemed annoyed by the humans and, slipping into the water with a single powerful tail-stroke, were gone.

Emerging from the mangroves was like arriving in paradise. After beaching their dinghy at the end of the river, the Sunderlands hiked across a sandy dune that led to the main attraction: the Aquarium. A shimmering turquoise inlet, the Aquarium's crystal waters were as clear as glass. A ring of sugar-white sand surrounded the inlet, and palm trees encircled the sand.

When the produce man arrived in his rickety truck, Marianne and Laurence gave the children *pesos* and watched the kind old man patiently teach the kids Spanish words for things like cabbage, carrots, and potatoes. Then, in Spanish, he would tell them the price and they would pay.

"Gracias, señor!" they'd chirp.

The Sunderlands loved watching their kids *live* life. There was no TV and there were no video games. Instead there were crocodiles and magnificent birds and people from other cultures, like the fruit and vegetable man with his colorful money and exotic names for ordinary things.

And with few stores and luxuries, the Sunderland kids learned a lesson Laurence and Marianne wanted them to learn from the beginning: to appreciate simple pleasures and, when no pleasures were readily apparent, to make do. For example, while cruising there weren't any bakeries with twenty kinds of donuts to choose from on a Saturday morning. Instead, there were dough balls with nutmeg in them. Marianne taught Abby how to puff them in the galley kitchen in a little simmering oil, then dust them with cinnamon and sugar. Not fancy, but a warm, sweet treat to remember.

 Those three years cruising with my family are some of my best memories. While we sailed between ports, we caught a lot of neat fish—really dazzling, gorgeous creatures that I've never seen even in a book. Dad would catch the biggest ones and carry them back to the cockpit and we would all stand around to see what he'd come up with that time. I remember one that looked like a parrot! Its skin shimmered with bright jungle colors and he even had a beak where his mouth should have been. Another time the catch of the day was a trumpet fish, which is super long and narrow with a funny little nose like a seahorse. One day Dad snagged a scary-looking specimen that had lips and teeth like a human being. Yuck! We named him the Tooth-Fish. Then we ate him for lunch.

We sailed from island to island, bay to bay, staying longer in the ones we liked best. Zac and I would be snorkeling, hiking, or running around the beach making new friends. On Sundays we tried to find a place to go to church. Let me tell you, in Mexico the locals are *serious* about church. I remember this one worship service in a town near Punta de Mita, just north of Puerto Vallarta, along what's called the Mexican Riviera. An American expatriate, along with about seventy other people including us, was having church literally in his backyard.

There were pigs snorting and rooting in a paddock and chickens running around between our legs. We were with the Swedbergs, a family we were buddy-boating with. Their sailboat was called *Fantasia*. The Swedbergs' son Karson played guitar while the local people sang praise songs in Spanish. Our friend Maria, a local woman who had lived in the States for a time and spoke fluent English, helped us along by translating. The people were so enthusiastic, singing and taking turns reading aloud from a Spanish translation of the Bible. We thought the service would last about two hours, but more than five hours later, backyard church was still going strong. The service went on so long that we missed the last bus back to Punta de Mita, so some of the church members drove us back to town in the back of their pickup truck. Totally illegal in the U.S., but in Mexico, a fun, dusty, bumpy ride!

While still anchored outside Punta de Mita, we got some terrible news. Our friend Captain Ron had been sailing his boat, *Still Crazy*, when he ran aground outside Punta de Mita. His boat was smashed into matchsticks. Captain Ron was banged up pretty badly and spent a few days in the hospital in Puerto Vallarta. He was an accomplished single-hander, and the news of his accident was a good teaching moment for my dad. He reminded us all that the ocean is boss and living on it requires vigilance at all times.

My favorite port was Tenacatita. Zac and I loved slowly motoring our dinghy up through the mangroves. The crocodiles weren't that big, maybe six or seven feet, and they would usually sit up on the banks in spots where the sun shined down through the jungle canopy. Sometimes it was a little scary when they slipped past us in the water because our dinghy was a boat with a hard bottom and inflatable sides that I didn't think would stand up very well to crocodile teeth.

Once, while bouncing across the bay in our dinghy on the way back to *Amazing Grace*, we saw a baby whale breaching, flying up and almost completely out of the water. It was late afternoon and the sun was already half-set. The baby itself was enormous, easily three times the size of our eight-foot dinghy, and its even bigger mom was swimming circles around him. This was the time in my life I was completely in love with all animals and convinced that I someday wanted to be a veterinarian or a zookeeper. Again and again, the baby exploded through the surface of the water and to me, being this close was better than Disneyland on the Fourth of July.

After each breach, the baby whale crashed down near its mother, sending a volcano blast of white foam into the air. Dad pulled closer and closer until we weren't more than forty feet from the two giant creatures. We all sat in silent awe until the baby breached, and it was like, wow! Then we sat quietly while Big Mama circled. No one wanted to get on the wrong side of Mama. Boats have been rammed by a mother whale when they got between her and her baby.

But these beautiful animals completely ignored us. The baby breached at least a dozen times. I've read some about why they do this. One theory says they're communicating, that the slap of their bodies against the water is a signal to other whales. Another theory is that when they breach, the big mammals are knocking barnacles off their skin. But to me that day, it looked like school. Again and again, the little whale leapt from the sea with its mom cutting circles around him. I imagined her coaching him underwater in whale-talk: "That was great, son! A little higher next time!"

Once we got back to *Amazing Grace*, I painted a watercolor of the baby whale's jumping practice. I sent it to my Grandpa Al in San Diego, who was a mechanical engineer. He took my little masterpiece to work and hung it up in his office.

We saw other cool creatures, too, like sharks, elephant seals, and sometimes sea turtles swimming at the surface with seagulls hitching rides on their backs. I remember these strange black birds with big red airbags under their chins, watching over little fuzzy babies in their nests. Other times, we saw iguanas three-feet long sunning themselves on the rocks of breakwaters.

Besides critters, we met all sorts of people like the Swedbergs, Captain Ron, and a salty lady named Diane who sailed alone with two huge parrots. Some boat people scrimped along, using chewing gum and wire to keep their vessels patched together. Then there were the rich powerboaters. They were used to being in big marinas and would sometimes roar into an anchorage with their huge engines, and were frowned on by the rest of us because of the nasty wakes they made.

Even though school wasn't my favorite thing, Mom made it fun by incorporating the animals we saw and the people we met into our homeschool lessons. If you think about it, cruising was like being on one long, giant field trip. I loved everything about it and so did my brothers and my sister. Living that way seemed so much more exciting than living in an ordinary house on an ordinary street. I loved the freedom and adventure of it, the warm and balmy islands, exotic creatures, "sand ball wars" with our cruising kid-friends on the beaches. Once you live like that, it's hard to go back to a "normal" life.

Still, when we first moved back into our house in Thousand Oaks, I was amazed at all the living space we had—I mean, I could do cartwheels in the house! Of course, we had to transition from boat-schooling to homeschooling. A lot of homeschoolers are really outgoing and everything and involved in a lot of different outside activities. I wasn't one of them. I was naturally shy, kind of antisocial, and didn't like speaking in public. Maybe that's why I started pouring a lot of time into raising animals.

It all started with a chicken.

Our neighbor gave us a chicken and my dad named it Gertrude. Before long we had a whole collection of chickens because my dad would go to the feed store and come home with a bunch of cute little fuzzy chicks and, of course, I thought they were adorable. We also got a couple of dogs, Queensland heelers named Sandy and Lacy, and some adorable dwarf bunnies, along with a huge rex rabbit that was about the size of a small child.

Then came the turkeys. Six of them.

By then I had gotten involved in the 4-H Club, and one day the leader of the group took delivery of a load of turkeys. Well, after about a week, she realized her daughter didn't have time to take care of the birds. So Dad being Dad said, "No worries! We'll take them!"

So now we had chickens, dogs, rabbits, and turkeys. It was fun, like having a little farm in our Southern California suburban backyard. Looking back, it didn't seem weird or nerdy at the time. Still, when Dad first said we'd take those turkeys, I thought he was nuts. But once I started entering my animals in competitions at 4-H fairs, I found out people pay big money for prize-winning animals. Three years in a row, I sold my champion turkeys at the 4-H auction. Even today, I couldn't tell you what makes a champion turkey, but I know this much: the first one sold for $500; the second for $600; and the third for $1,200! I was thirteen years old with $2,300 in the bank.

About a year later, I used my turkey money to buy my own horse. I had wanted a horse ever since I was five years old. Mom and Dad heard about a horse for sale, so we went to look at him. He was a retired show horse, a sleek brown Russian Arabian warm blood with a black mane.

His name was Czar—perfect! We were able to stable him across the street with neighbors who also had a couple of horses. Their backyard was big enough for a small barn. I went over every day to groom and feed Czar, and rode him about every other day. Often I rode him over to our house and gave my little brothers and sisters rides.

You have to picture this. We do not live on a country road. It's just a regular suburban street. I always got a lot of funny looks, because here I was trotting around the neighborhood, usually bareback, with cars pulling in and out of driveways honking, and little kids running after me, yelling, "My turn! Me next!"

Looking back on it all—the family cruising, the 4-H fairs, the animals, growing up in a great big family—it was a pretty cool childhood. Pretty perfect, actually. Still, after a while, I started to feel restless, like I was doing and seeing the same things over and over again.

Then when I was thirteen, Dad started having me help him deliver boats. Not tow them somewhere on a trailer, but actually sail or motor from one port to another. I absolutely loved it. And even though our house was big and the boats were small, it wasn't long before houses and buildings and streets started to make me feel almost claustrophobic. After that it seemed that no matter how much I enjoyed life at home, the sea always called me back.

One day that same year, I told my dad that someday, I would sail around the world alone. Fewer people have successfully solo-circumnavigated the globe than have journeyed into space, so Dad didn't jump right on board with the idea. But he didn't treat it like a joke, either.

"Let's just see how things go," he said.

CHAPTER 2

ABBY'S DREAM

MARINA DEL REY AND THOUSAND OAKS, CALIFORNIA
2006

 One day when I was still thirteen, Dad had to deliver two boats on the same day, from Ventura to Marina del Rey. At first I was going to sail with him, but instead I ended up skippering one of the boats on my own. My good friend Kasey Nash came along for company.

It was about a forty-mile trip. Once both boats were safely tied up at Marina del Rey, my dad asked me, "So, how did you feel about it?"

"Piece of cake, Dad," I said. "I've been sailing with you all my life."

For me, a day on the water was every bit as normal as a day ashore.

That same day, Dad and I made another two-boat delivery, this time from Long Beach back to Marina del Rey, about thirty more miles. Dad was sailing the sloop ahead of me, and we were delivering both vessels to a boat show. The skies had become low and gray and foggy, with icy winds and churning waves hitting my boat right on the nose. White water smashed over my bow and beam, and the boat slammed hard across the waves, sounding like it was going to break apart. By the time night fell, I had been hand steering for a total of twelve hours that day. It was a strenuous, exhausting job, like running a marathon. I was soaked through, freezing cold, teeth chattering.

I was absolutely miserable . . . but I loved it.

Kind of weird, but true. When you're sailing, it's always in the back of your mind that terrible things can happen. The mental process is to view it as a challenge. I learned early how to do that. That night, I had two choices: I could either shrink back against the power of the wind and sea, or I could mentally pump my fist in the air and meet the challenge head-on.

I decided to do it the second way. In the end, when I stepped off that boat dripping wet and freezing, I felt good about having gone through something tough and coming out on top of it. And I felt good about the way I'd handled it. You can go through tough circumstances and come out on top, but how you handle the in-between, that's what makes you the person you are. My parents taught me that.

The sloop Laurence Sunderland was sailing ahead of his daughter that night had all the luxuries aboard and a great big dodger, a kind of Plexiglas awning that shields the cockpit against the worst of the weather. Even with all that and his decades at sea, *he* was uncomfortable. Abby had had to hand steer for thirty miles through heavy seas and a lashing storm. As they pounded up the coast, he looked back at her boat and could see the mast light arcing back and forth through the dark, which meant her boat was rocking gunwale to gunwale. Waves smashed over his own beam—the side of the boat—so he knew his daughter had to be standing astride the deck in a wide stance, holding on to the wheel, heeling over all the way to port, then all the way to starboard.

For a father it was a moment of terror and a moment of pride. *Man, he thought, she's hanging in there. She's actually doing this.*

Of course, doing it and liking it are two different things. Rides like that have unveiled men who thought they were old salts as fair weather sailors. Sailing is "fun" until you have a ride where you feel as if you're going to be thrown out of the boat every second, no matter how hard you hold on.

Yes, Laurence thought, *this trip might possibly cure Abby of this notion she has of sailing around the world.*

After a sail like that, most people tied up to a dock sputtering, "I never knew it was going to be *that* horrible! Get me off this boat!"

Not Abby. She wrestled her boat to the dock a few minutes behind Laurence, tossed him a line, and climbed out onto the dock. Soaking wet, she looked up at her father, eyes shining with happiness. Laurence stood there in amazement. His daughter, now almost fourteen years old, had just popped out of a pounding, freezing sea and was clearly full of joy. He realized that something deep inside her was coming to the surface and thought for the first time, *She might possibly have what it takes to do this.*

In addition to expert seamanship, what it takes is a tenacious spirit, being levelheaded in adversity, and the mechanical knowledge to be able to work through difficulties. As far as Laurence was concerned, another requirement was key: devotion to God. Having been in some life-or-death situations, he knew that the sea takes people beyond their comfort zones, into a place where there is only one Source of help. All the ingenuity, all the high-tech gear, all the jury-rigging—sometimes the sea would rip it all away until there was only you, the Creator, and His mercy.

That it was a great and changing Unknown was one of the things Laurence had learned to love about the sea. Although it covers 70 percent of the planet's surface, it is a place that not a lot of people get to see. There are spots on the earth that no man can touch or set foot on unless they cross vast blue expanses in a boat.

There's a chameleon mystique about the ocean, Laurence felt. It really is alive. Not just alive with sea life, but alive in itself. It is the seedbed of the earth's weather. Ninety percent of all volcanic activity emanates from the ocean floors. The sea contains almost two hundred thousand identified species, but scientists believe there are more than three times that many marine species living out of human view.

The longest mountain range on earth is actually underwater. The mid-ocean range winds around the entire globe from the Arctic Ocean to the Atlantic, beneath the hem of Africa, Asia, and Australia, and across the Pacific Ocean to the North American coast. It is four times longer than the Himalayas, Rockies, and Andes combined. The ocean is home to the largest living structure on earth—the Great Barrier Reef, which is more than fourteen hundred miles long and can be seen from space.

Still, for all its majesty, Laurence Sunderland maintained a love/ hate relationship with the sea. There were some times when he gloried in every salty, crashing wave and other times when he wished he'd never set foot on a boat.

All this flashed through Laurence's mind in a second as he and Abby stood on the frigid dock that night. But he didn't let it show on his face. Instead, he looked down at his daughter and said with a teaspoon of irony, "So, Abby, are you still ready to sail around the world?"

"Show me my boat," she said with a grin. "I'm ready to go."

CHAPTER 3
BOAT HUNTING

THOUSAND OAKS, CALIFORNIA
2008–2009

 The Sunderlands had read many biographies of sailors and explorers, especially when they were sailing in Mexico. Thematically, it just fit with the homeschooling and all the traveling. One of the kids' favorite books was *The Boy Who Sailed Around the World Alone* by Robin Lee Graham, who had sailed around the world as a teen. Graham also wrote a memoir for adults called *Dove*, but the kids loved the first title because it featured lots of colorful and unusual pictures of Graham exploring little islands and exotic countries, meeting local people and living among them. The stories fired the Sunderland kids' imaginations and expanded their idea of what was possible—and when.

In 2008, after ten years of homeschooling, the Sunderlands decided to enroll Zac in a private Christian college-prep school to play football. He did extremely well, was named Most Valuable Player on defense, and he was making good grades. But he also fell in with some kids whose activities didn't mesh with Zac's natural gifts, like a solid work ethic and self-discipline. As a homeschooler he had learned to apply himself to his responsibilities; in that environment, the sooner you get your work done, the sooner you can go do something fun. The crowd he fell in with was more into cheating and goofing off. It was when the Sunderlands found out there was some experimentation with drugs that they pulled Zac out of the school.

With football behind him, Zac, an athlete with a brain, found himself at loose ends. Laurence and Marianne began praying that he would develop a passion, a goal, something he could pour himself into. During that time Zac watched a documentary called *Deep Water*. The film was about Donald Crowhurst, a British weekend sailor and inventor, who entered the Golden Globe race in 1968, hoping the prize money and publicity would save him from financial ruin.

The Golden Globe is no longer running, but the race rules then required that each entrant set sail between June 1 and October 31 so that they could pass through the dangerous Southern Ocean during summer. In addition to Crowhurst, seven other competitors entered the race, including Nigel Tetley, a lieutenant commander in the Royal Navy, and Robin Knox-Johnston, who had served in the Royal Navy and Merchant Marines.

Crowhurst set sail on the last possible day, Halloween 1968. His boat, *Teignmouth Electron*, was a forty-foot trimaran. Crowhurst immediately ran into trouble and decided to falsify his logs to make it appear that he had completed the race. For months he sailed erratically around the Southern Atlantic, calling in false progress reports and faking his logs. He also spent a lot of time in radio silence, leaving race watchers to extrapolate his position from his last known report. Crowhurst's plan was to rejoin the race in such a way as to come in last in elapsed time. He figured that his logs wouldn't be scrutinized as carefully as if he were a front-runner.

Ironically, based on his deception, Crowhurst was soon being hailed as the likely winner of the race. But his lies had near-fatal consequences for Nigel Tetley. He had long since sailed past Crowhurst's hiding place, but based on Crowhurst's false reports, believed himself to be in a dead heat for the "elapsed time" first-place finish. Tetley's boat was failing, but he pushed himself on and was eventually forced to abandon ship.

All of these events took a toll on Crowhurst. His last radio transmission was June 29, 1969. His last log entry was dated July 1. Nine days later, the *Teignmouth Electron* was found abandoned and adrift, with three log books, a radio log, and other papers aboard. Crowhurst's log revealed a rapid mental breakdown, with false entries, real ones, random irrational thoughts, and writings that revealed his agony over the possibility of being declared the winner. If he won, his logs would be closely examined, exposing his deception and adding humiliation to financial ruin. Historians believe Crowhurst committed suicide by jumping into the sea.

In the end, Robin Knox-Johnston won the race. Though he lost his self-steering gear off Australia, he finished on April 22, 1969, becoming the first man to circumnavigate the globe nonstop and single-handed. He donated his prize money to the widow and daughter of Donald Crowhurst and, for his achievement in sailing, was named a Commander of the Order of the British Empire by Queen Elizabeth II.

After the movie, Laurence and Marianne were in their room getting ready for bed. Zac walked in and said, "I could do that."

"Do what?" Laurence asked.

"I could sail around the world."

Laurence and Marianne looked at each other. Maybe this was the answer to their prayer. Perhaps Zac had found a focus, a place to pour his passion.

The Sunderlands had been frugal with their money. Over the years, they had managed to sock away a healthy savings account, and they owned their Thousand Oaks home outright—both unusual circumstances in the era of mountainous credit card debt and mortgaged

McMansions. So when it turned out that hundreds of sponsorship appeals yielded zero results, the Sunderlands decided to finance Zac's trip themselves on the condition that he pay them back over time.

With his own savings Zac purchased an Islander 36 called *Intrepid*, got a support team together, and preparation for his 2008–2009 campaign began. Abby was fourteen at the time and her little brother, Ben, was just a baby, so she stayed home a lot helping her mom. Still, Marianne noticed Abby following preparations for Zac's solo-round try with keen interest.

"Don't even ask, cause it's not gonna happen," Marianne told her more than once.

"Yes it is!" Abby would say, laughing.

"No," Marianne would say seriously. "It's not."

But after Zac returned from his trip—complete with tales of exotic ports, friendly people, long days alone at sea, and a brush with pirates near Indonesia—Abby got more and more serious. Since those first solo boat deliveries when she was thirteen, Abby had helped with many more deliveries. She loved sailing alone, skippering her own boat. And the worse the conditions, the better she liked it.

Then one day, Laurence came to Marianne and said, "She wants to go."

After eighteen years of marriage, Marianne was used to Laurence's big dreams for his family. Some of them, like the three years they'd spent cruising, panned out. Others, like Laurence's dream to build a cabin in the wilderness and move the family there, didn't. It was clear that the idea of sending Abby around the world was a long shot. The Sunderlands had spent their life savings on Zac's trip, and without a sponsor there was no question about Abby going. Financially, the trip would be out of the question.

"Why don't we put out a press release announcing Abby's intentions and see if we can get a sponsor?" Marianne said. That was her ace in the hole, Marianne thought: *She'll never get a sponsor and that will be the end of it.*

It wasn't that she didn't think Abby had the sailing skills to make a solo try; it was just that she didn't yet feel up to the hard work of another solo-round campaign, not to mention the sleepless nights wondering if her child was okay.

The next week, Marianne called a friend, Christian Pinkston, who had handled Zac's PR when he completed his trip. Christian wrote a press release and sent it out. The very next day, the Sunderland's phone rang.

It was Shoe City, offering a major sponsorship for Abby.

 Wow! I could hardly believe it when Shoe City came aboard as a major sponsor. Just like that, what had seemed like only a dream began to seem closer to reality.

At first my dad thought about designing the ideal boat for me to sail, one that was fast but safe, similar to an Open 40. The open class boats are racing boats, but built with better safety features. In the past, designers had been so intent on speed that they'd sometimes compromised structural soundness. Some vessels were losing their keels, or literally cracking under the pressure of overly tight rigging and sails that caught too much wind. The boat Dad had in mind would have incorporated the open class safety features along with some added luxuries. But since the weather window for me to take the Southern Ocean route was closing fast, it would've been unrealistic for Dad to work with marine architects to build a custom boat.

After doing some research online, Dad consulted Dawn Riley, one of the foremost sailors in the world. Dawn suggested that we contact an expert named Troy Bethel, who had a lot of experience with the open-style race boats. Dad and Troy discussed which of two kinds of vessels would be best for my trip. The first, called "heavy displacement" boats, are slower, but generally thought to be safer because of their higher stability. The second kind—the Open 40s, 50s, 60s, and 70s—are kind of like sleds. My dad didn't have a lot of experience with the open boats, but Troy had sailed them in the Southern Ocean, and also owned an Open 50, which he kept in Marina del Rey.

After weighing the open boats against the heavy displacement option, Troy, Dad, and I decided that the open-style was the safer option. My solo circumnavigation route would take me through both the churning waters below Cape Horn and the massive waves of the Southern Ocean. In high seas, heavy displacement boats are more likely to get "pooped on"—it really *is* called that!—when waves break over the stern again and again, finally filling up the cockpit, and sometimes swamping the boat. But the open boats' sledlike hull and massive sails are designed to surf down the wave fronts just ahead of the breaks. The opens are also a lot faster, which means they are better able to outrun storm systems. Having a faster boat also meant spending less time in the dangerous Southern Ocean.

While Dad and I researched boats, I spent September 2009 in constant training, both on and off the water. Even sailing with a crew is physically strenuous. Sailing alone, I would need to build as much muscle as possible. Sid Wing, a sailor and good family friend, set up a gym workout for me. It included a lot of upper-body training since my trip would require that kind of strength for handling my boat in heavy winds. Sid also put me on a running regimen. To tell you the truth, I hated the running, but I did it because I needed to build not only strength, but also endurance. Later, as my voyage unfolded, I would be really glad I stuck with the training program.

Although I had extensive sailing experience, now that I was actively planning my solo circumnavigation on an Open 40, I needed more experience on the open-style boats. So I started sailing *Nanuq*, Troy's Open 50. It was pretty much the same vessel I'd be using for my solo-round, just ten feet longer. *Nanuq* was a fast, sleek sports car of a boat. After sailing her several times, I didn't think I'd ever be able to go back to sailing cruisers, which now seemed to me big, slow, and clunky. Another benefit of sailing with Troy was the chance for him to download all the stuff he knew about the Southern Ocean. He talked about what it was like down there, the strain on the boat, and the work I would need to do to keep up with it. Troy really helped me to know what to expect.

My brother Zac had completed his thirteen-month circumnavigation in July 2009. He helped me prepare for my trip two ways. First, by teaching me the strategies he'd learned for safety, navigation, and getting some sleep between blows and inevitable equipment breakdowns. And second, by teasing me until I was ready to choke him.

While all this was going on, Dad and I found two boats we thought might work. One, called *Wild Eyes*, was for sale in Rhode Island with a price tag of $150,000. An Open 40 that had already completed a successful circumnavigation, she was advertised as a turnkey boat— ship-shape and "ready to go" around the world again. The other boat, a Class 40 (very similar to an Open 40), was in Nassau, Bahamas. At around $250,000, it cost way more than *Wild Eyes*, but it had also recently been refitted, so Dad and Troy thought it was worth a look.

Tapping into the Shoe City sponsorship money for plane tickets, Dad, Troy, Sid, and I flew out to Rhode Island to look at *Wild Eyes*. I had seen the pictures of her online and was super excited. Originally named *BTC Velocity*, the boat was designed by Scott Jutson, an Australian yacht designer who is famous for a string of "firsts." His "maxi yacht"—or large racing boat—*Brindabella*, broke and still holds the most Australian East Coast racing records. He also designed the boat sailed by the first Malaysian to single-hand around the world.

Best of all, *Wild Eyes* had already proved she could successfully circle the globe. Alan Paris completed the 2002 Around Alone on her, becoming the first Bermudan to solo circumnavigate. Paris completed the course—from Newport, Rhode Island/New York, to Brixham, Devon, to Cape Town to Tauranga to Salvador, Brazil, and back to Newport—in 202 days.

After a six-hour cross-country flight, we landed in Rhode Island, rented a car, and drove straight to the marina. I could hardly wait to get there! I had read so much about *Wild Eyes* on the Internet and I was super excited about getting out there and sailing her. I really hoped she was the right boat for me.

But when we got to the marina, my heart dropped into my stomach. Instead of a race car, we found . . . well, a fixer-upper. The deck paint was worn and cracked in places. The solar panel covers were coming apart. Much of the rigging would have to be pulled and replaced. There was even a bit of delamination, meaning the core of the hull was separating from the Kevlar outer skin, and that was a serious issue.

Considering the way *Wild Eyes* had been advertised, my dad was not at all happy to find the boat in the shape it was in. "You've misrepresented this boat," he said to the broker. "It's definitely not 'ready to go.' It's old, tired, and worn out."

I don't even remember the rest of the conversation, only that we got back on a plane and flew home. We were all super disappointed that we had spent precious time and sponsorship money. I was also disappointed that I still didn't have a boat.

This part—the waiting, the hoping, the *praying*—was probably one of the hardest parts of my trip. The Shoe City sponsorship was huge and generous. But it was not enough to purchase the Nassau boat, much less cover the rest of the costs associated with a solo-round campaign. We had been incredibly blessed that Shoe City stepped up so quickly. When Zac decided to sail the world, he sent out hundreds of letters requesting sponsorship. He got some good equipment sponsors, but no one willing to put their name on his boat.

Flying west toward home, I wondered, what were the chances that I would get not just one generous sponsor, but two?

We could afford *Wild Eyes*, though, and after we got back to Thousand Oaks, Dad and Troy talked seriously about a plan to refit her. But as weeks passed, her owner started playing hardball. If we didn't buy her soon, he said, he might take her off the market. If that happened and we didn't find another major sponsor so that we could buy the Nassau boat, the whole trip could fall apart for lack of funding.

The waiting was terrible. I wanted to break the record, of course, and become the youngest person to sail around the world solo and unassisted. But I also simply wanted to sail around the world. I knew if this trip collapsed, I'd definitely be trying again in 2011. Still, after all the excitement, training, and anticipation, the thought of being stuck at home, doing schoolwork, and living a completely normal life was something I was definitely not interested in.

On September 7, 2009, my dad and Sid flew down to Nassau to check out the Class 40. She was in great condition, and they actually sailed her about a hundred miles before Dad decided there were a couple of reasons he didn't think the vessel was right for my campaign. First, she had a very wide, very open cockpit. In the rough waters around Cape Horn and all throughout the Southern Ocean, Dad thought something more snug would mean less chance of me being thrown out. The Nassau boat also had fewer watertight bulkheads— walls that divide the hull into independent compartments—than Dad thought were important for safety and structural soundness in a solo-round attempt.

So Dad and Sid rejected that vessel and flew back to California, which meant I still didn't have a boat. But there was also another hitch in the plan: my mom.

 Marianne Sunderland had long been fairly vocal about her opposition to Abby's campaign, even from the time Abby had begun suggesting it nearly three years before. But once the sponsorship came through, the fuse was lit, and Laurence was so busy racing forward that he and Marianne didn't discuss Abby's campaign much—especially since Marianne had been the one who had suggested seeking sponsorship.

Still, as Abby's training and the boat hunt commenced, Marianne did feel a bit left behind. She knew she was married to an adventurous, enthusiastic man who dreamed a bit bigger than most men. Sometimes he let his enthusiasm get out ahead of him and that was okay; it was part of Laurence's charm.

After he returned from Nassau, Laurence sensed disharmony with his wife. He realized he had not been considerate about including her in the decision making, and found himself at a crossroads. On the weekend of October 17, Laurence pulled Marianne into their bedroom and shut the door. "Look, I know we've been running ahead with this, but if you're not on board, we're not going forward," he said. "We need to be one. We're either all in or all out. If you don't want Abby to do this, we'll give all the money back and stop this right now."

Marianne was torn. *Oh great*, she thought. *I get to be the great big wet blanket.*

On the other hand, she appreciated Laurence's gesture and, after eighteen years of marriage, knew it to be genuine. Knowing that he was willing to give it up if she wasn't 100 percent behind the campaign gave her comfort.

For his part, Laurence realized when undertaking something this big, the whole family needed to pull in the same direction. Even more than that, they needed to know they were in unison in their prayer life. "If the Lord wasn't with us," he would later say, "we might as well give up from the get-go."

So there in the bedroom that day, Laurence said, "Let's take the weekend and pray about it."

That Saturday and Sunday, the Sunderlands kicked back and didn't do much outside of going to church and seeking God in prayer. Marianne knew Abby would be disappointed—crushed even—if she, Marianne, emerged from the weekend saying no to the round-the-world trip. But Marianne wasn't afraid to say no. With seven kids and one on the way, she was an old hand at mothering and didn't care one lick if one of her kids was mad at her for a day or a week or a month. She was the mom, Abby was the kid, and that was that.

Also, Marianne really appreciated Laurence putting the brakes on. He had come to her and let her know in no uncertain terms that if she said no to Abby's trip, he would support her; it would be communicated as a joint decision—not with Mom as the bad guy. Seeing that her husband was balanced about the idea and truly willing to give it up altogether freed Marianne to really speak her mind.

After that weekend, she still had concerns over whether was Abby mature enough to handle the journey. But Marianne also realized that Laurence was a marine expert who'd just successfully sent their oldest son around the world, and who loved their oldest daughter as much as she did. Also, Abby had been training diligently, and God seemed to be opening doors and providing in so many ways. Finally, if the trip wasn't going well, or if it turned out that long months alone at sea weren't Abby's cup of tea, she could always put in at Chile or the Falklands or Cape Town and call it a wrap.

Marianne also reflected on how much Zac's trip had impacted his Christian beliefs. Before his sail, Zac seemed to have been slipping the moorings of his faith. But he had returned from his journey praising God for what He had done in his life. At a press conference, Zac told reporters, "I don't know if any of you out there are atheists, but God answered so many of my prayers while I was out there that it's impossible for me to believe that there is no God."

In the end, Marianne decided that no matter what happened, if they reminded people of what the Sunderland family based their lives on—their faith in God—that Abby's trip would be a success.

With the Nassau boat a no-go, the only yacht to sort out was *Wild Eyes*. Yes, she'd need a lot of work, the Sunderlands agreed. But what she did have was perfect for Abby's campaign. *Wild Eyes* was part of a new generation of single-handed boats designed to meet new international standards for self-righting and flotation. To meet those standards, Scott Jutson's design had to prove that the skipper could "re-right" the boat from 180 degrees, using water ballast. In other words, if *Wild Eyes* was completely upside down in the water, the skipper had to be able to pull her completely upright—deck up, keel down—and do it alone.

To achieve this, Jutson incorporated into his design water ballast and an unstable inverted shape. That meant that if *Wild Eyes* was rotated deck-down in the water, her unusual shape caused her to naturally continue the rotation in the direction of bottom-heavy water ballast held in the lower parts of the hull.

Another of the new safety features was "positive flotation." *Wild Eyes* was fitted with so much buoyant material that she could keep afloat 130 percent of her own body weight. It would be like strapping 130 pounds of Styrofoam to a 100-pound man and throwing him into the sea: As long as he stayed with the Styrofoam, he would be unsinkable.

In an article discussing his design, Scott Jutson put it this way: "In short, regardless of what catastrophe hit the boat, it would remain afloat."[1]

Wild Eyes had some other amazing safety features: she had five watertight bulkheads, or walls, which meant that if one part of the hull was somehow pierced or damaged, only a portion of the boat would flood, not the whole thing. She also had a tear-away bow section so that in a collision the rest of the boat, including the cockpit and cabin, would remain afloat. Her steel keel was designed to withstand high-speed grounding without tearing out the bottom of the hull, and her rig—the mast and its components—was designed for extra stability in extreme conditions. The way Laurence and Troy saw it, sending Abby to sea in *Wild Eyes* would be like sending her in an unsinkable tank. Laurence knew that as long as his daughter stayed with the boat, she'd be just fine.

CHAPTER 4

WILD EYES

EASTERN SEABOARD AND ENSENADA, MEXICO
2009

 On October 19, 2009, my sixteenth birthday, *Wild Eyes* officially became mine! We had negotiated the price down to $90,000, and the moment Dad signed the papers was without a doubt the most exciting moment to that point in my life. I had begun to believe that dreams were meant to be no more than dreams, and that in the real world, dreams don't come true. Then Zac left on his trip, and it was amazing to see all the support he got from around the world. Watching him complete his solo-round inspired me to believe I could do it, too. And now I had *Wild Eyes*. Now it was really happening.

In Newport, Rhode Island, Dad surveyed the boat to see what all she needed. Obviously, we weren't going to refit her completely there. After researching a couple of options for transporting *Wild Eyes* to the West Coast—by truck across the states or by ship out of Rhode

Island—it became clear that only one option would meet our timeline. We would sail her to Fort Lauderdale, Florida. There she would be loaded aboard a freighter and transported through the Panama Canal and on up the coast to Ensenada, Mexico.

But even to sail *Wild Eyes* down the Eastern Seaboard, we had to make sure of a couple of basics. Dad bought and installed brand-new batteries and made sure the alternators were in good shape. He also repaired a couple of communications issues.

While waiting for our weather window to set sail from Newport, we went to a gathering at a little pub near the waterfront, as guests of Trond Hjerto, a Norwegian skipper we'd met on the marina. Trond was an interesting-looking guy, on the shorter side with a great big beard. He reminded us of a smallish Viking. While we waited out the weather, Trond let us stay on his boat. That's one of the really cool things about the sailing life—all the cool people you meet, and how quickly you form friendships because of your common bond with the sea. Before we left Newport, Trond gave me a copy of *The Hobbit*, by J. R. R. Tolkien. He said it would be a good book to read on my sail.

On November 1, we got underway. We left Newport Harbor in flukey winds on the tail end of a front. *Wild Eyes* was a little challenging to handle in the shifting winds, but gradually we got to know her. Once we got out on the open ocean, though, she sailed like a dream. Then on our second day out, we got a bit of a blow and were absolutely flying down these really big seas. It was just incredible!

Wild Eyes was a little tender or "tippy," but she also handled winds with ease. When you're sailing in a bay, you might sail out and tack back five or ten miles. But when you're sailing distances, you may be on one tack—a certain alignment of the sails with the wind—for a long period of time. *Wild Eyes* handled the winds beautifully, and also turned out to be quite forgiving in some ways. For example, in strong gusts of wind or building conditions, when reefing (reducing the amount of sail area) was necessary, she would simply spill air rather than holding on to it. In similar conditions a lot of boats would have "rounded up"—or headed up into the wind and slowed or stalled out. But *Wild Eyes* was so strong and well designed that she sailed easily through conditions that might have given lesser boats trouble. The more I sailed her, the more I fell in love.

The trip to Fort Lauderdale was a neat experience for Dad. All our lives, sailing as a family, he had been in charge. While Zac and I helped out, Dad was always the official skipper. But this sail was different. Zac had sailed around the world and I had a few more miles under my belt, so Dad was there for support in case we needed it. But mostly he took a back seat and let us drive. The whole trip was great for me to learn *Wild Eyes'* systems and how to sail her in various kinds of weather. It became even clearer to me just how much work she would be to handle. She was designed for single-handing but was still a race boat. Her large sail area made for great speeds but also meant she took much more work to control. Going fast is great, but on a race boat, when things start going bad they go bad fast.

Our Eastern Seaboard sail gave Dad a ton of confidence both in me and in the boat. Sailors headed south along the East Coast try to avoid sailing against the Gulf Stream, a powerful, warm current that starts in the Gulf of Mexico and rushes north along the U.S. East Coast. Add in a storm or a gale, then the skies go dark and the seas can get steep, choppy, and "confused," meaning that waves can come from all different directions. When Dad saw how well *Wild Eyes* handled those conditions and different "points of sail"—or wind angles—he told me it gave him great peace of mind that we had chosen the right boat. In fact, at one point conditions were so rough that a Coast Guard helicopter flew out, hovered over our position, and radioed us. They were looking for a vessel that had called in a distress signal. Were we that boat, they wanted to know?

"No, it's not us," Dad said. "We're doing fine."

Well, except maybe for the "head," the sailor's term for "toilet." Heads are always breaking down, and on our third day out, ours did, too, and it was unfixable. So for the next couple of days, we had to use the "bucket and chuck it" method. Yuck.

On our way to Fort Lauderdale, we made two stops: once in Fort Pierce to fix the head (quite a relief!) and then in West Palm to untangle a crab-pot line that had wrapped around the propeller and fouled the shaft, strut, and stern tube.

I feel it's important to mention that the broken head and fouled engine were nothing compared to sailing with Captain Zac. He took advantage of the fact that there were no mirrors on the boat, so there was rarely a day when I didn't walk around for hours with some kind of artwork on my face that he'd managed to draw on me while I slept. He also took great joy in little things, like my being mortified as I watched him wash out a drinking cup with saltwater and a dirty sock. Still, Zac was great crew, even if he was a really annoying big brother.

Even before she was hoisted aboard the freighter in Fort Lauderdale, we started refitting *Wild Eyes*. The ship wouldn't sail for another five days, and Dad wanted to get right to work. Using sponsorship money from Shoe City, we bought and installed two wind generators along with their monitoring systems. We also put in all-new solar panels and a Ray Marine chart plotter.

After the Panama Canal, *Wild Eyes'* first stop was the Baja beach town of Ensenada, Mexico. Ensenada is far enough south in Baja to be away from the busy border towns, but still close enough for Americans to road-trip down there for Pacific lobster served Mexican-style with refried beans and tortillas. Dad and Zac drove down on Thursday, December 3. I sailed down with friend and team member, Pieter Kokelaar, arriving the next day.

By the time *Wild Eyes* made it to the West Coast, my trip had started to attract some media attention. Pete Thomas, Shachi Cunningham, and Al Scheib, all from the *Los Angeles Times*, drove down together in Pete's car. They met Zac and me on the docks in Ensenada, along with photographer Lisa Gizara, who had become a good friend to us during Zac's trip.

The day was warm and sunny. We could see the freighter anchored inside the harbor just across the marina. The procedure was supposed to happen like this: The ship would come a certain distance into the harbor, then lower *Wild Eyes* into the water. After that we'd motor her in. But the "launch" time, as it's called, kept getting pushed back. And the farther it got pushed, and the longer I stood on that dock staring at my boat *this close,* the more impatient I got. It was worse than waiting for Christmas! (Although, since I was getting a $90,000 boat on December 3, I wasn't expecting anything for Christmas, anyway!)

Finally, we could see the ship's crew beginning to move *Wild Eyes.* The whole crowd of us—me, Zac, Lisa, and the *L.A. Times* crew—piled into a panga and motored over to the ship. Watching her lowered into the water was a big moment for me. It was as though the instant she touched the blue Pacific, my dream became real.

Once the ship's crew detached the sling, we all hopped from the panga to *Wild Eyes.* After a few cranks of her dormant engine, I was able to get her started, and we motored over to the dock to pick up Dad, who had been "enjoying" himself with customs officials for the past four hours.

Ensenada to San Diego, the southernmost American port on the West Coast, would be a sixty-three mile sail—about a twelve-hour run. Quite a trip for the time of year, but the *Times* crew seemed up for it, so off we went. We sailed out of Ensenada's harbor at about noon hoping to make San Diego by midnight. We started off with a zippy little wind, but slowly I watched our speed fall until finally the wind died almost completely. Midnight came and went and, one by one, our passengers headed below to try to get some sleep. Dad and I spent the night topside keeping an eye out for crab pots and kelp, and talking about the work to be done.

I love sailing with my dad. I remember that back in our cruising days, some families would crash their dinghies on the beach while trying to go ashore. But we never did. Back then, I thought it was cool having a dad who knew what he was doing on the water. Now, sailing *Wild Eyes* north through the night, I got that same feeling. With my dad, I always felt safe.

We pulled into San Diego at 6:00 a.m. and disembarked the worn-out *Times* team. After a night crammed in a cabin built for one, they were all great sports, but still glad to be ashore, I think. Then Dad and I cleared customs, fueled up, and set sail for our home port of Marina del Rey.

CHAPTER 5
RACEBOAT REFIT

MARINA DEL REY, CALIFORNIA
OCTOBER–DECEMBER 2009

 Back in Marina del Rey, we plunged into the refit with both feet—dozens of feet actually, as my dad tapped friends and experts from all over the sailing community. For weeks we were up before dawn and home after dark. By December 11, *Wild Eyes* looked like a beehive with workers swarming all over her. Nacho, a fiberglass and E-glass specialist, had his workers down below cutting delaminated fiberglass out of the hull. Alan Blunt, the rigger, was poring over the rigging looking for the tiniest flaws. Although the rigging would have to be pulled, and most of the running and standing rigging replaced, Alan said it was in good condition overall. The whole crew that had pitched in knew that time was short, and they worked like maniacs to get the refit done.

The hull delamination was repaired . . . C&C Marine overhauled the engine and installed new alternators . . . we had a stainless steel arch built and mounted to the aft end of the boat to house the solar panels and two wind generators . . . a new bilge pump and alarm system were installed . . . we installed new nonskid on the decks and repainted them . . . the charging systems were redesigned, installed, and tested. Alan Metzger, a yacht owner from Ventura, volunteered for the team and installed a new water maker. We also had the winches serviced and had all electrical, mechanical, and electronics systems tested.

Our friend, electrical engineer Mike Smith, installed all new wiring for two wind generators and two independent solar systems (these would charge all my battery-powered gear—satellite phones, radios, radar, autopilot) so that I wouldn't have to rely entirely on my engine. It was a backed-up back-up power system. Jerry Nash, a good friend and former Alaskan fisherman, worked tirelessly to fix the diesel cabin heater, a critical piece of gear I knew I'd rely on heavily in the freezing southern latitudes. The initial plan was for Jerry to spend a few days cleaning up some of the cabin wiring, but after he got going, he spent several weeks cleaning up raceways; installing pumps, new battery cables and switches; repairing navigation lights and reworking engine harnesses.

Unless you've been involved with this kind of voyage, it's hard to imagine the amount of work that goes into preparing for one. Big jobs like those already mentioned all bring with them tons of details that need attention. As my launch date neared, many boat experts volunteered their time and effort to help. Brady Nash, a friend who had commercially fished in Alaska for years, was eager to be part of my adventure. He pulled wires, gathered tools, and generally volunteered for anything that needed doing. Pieter Kokelaar, who had been in Ensenada with us, berthed his boat, *Lady K*, near *Wild Eyes* so that he could be instantly available to help other workers when needed. Pieter had spent time as a ship's engineer, wedging himself into tight spaces to check and repair gear. Crawling around and working in *Wild Eyes'* tiny compartments reminded him of those days, he said, except for the fact that it was easier when he was younger.

UK-Halsey, the oldest international sailmaking group, made the sails for *Wild Eyes*. The company had also made the sails for my brother's trip, and Dad really trusted them. My sails had to be tough enough to make the whole trip nonstop in extreme conditions, yet light enough for me to handle them. That led us to choose UK-Halsey's Spectra Tape-Drive sails. They are shaped with crosscut panels of a fiercely strong laminate, then reinforced with a grid of carbon fiber tape. I knew I would never have to worry about their performance.

The weather stayed on our side and by December 22, *Wild Eyes* was dressed out in her new paint scheme, with her Shoe City logo, big green *I Dream of Jeannie* eyes on her hull, and a bright white bottom. We decided that if she ever lost her keel and flipped upside down, *Wild Eyes'* white bottom would be pretty much impossible to spot from the air. We first decided to paint a big orange circle on the bottom, but then changed our minds and painted a great big heart. It looked pretty cool, but I was hoping no one would ever have to see it.

Right around this time, a no-kidding genius named Jeff Casher came aboard as a permanent part of the team. He and his wife, Gail, lived at the marina on their forty-six-foot cruising sailboat, *Sea Witch*. Laurence knew that the Cashers had spent eight years circumnavigating the globe. They had done it in a seriously see-the-world way, visiting fifty-five countries, including Borneo (where they traveled two days upriver to see the orangutans); Seba (where they visited an animist village right out of *Clan of the Cave Bear*); and Vanuatu (where cannibalism was "officially" stopped in 1969, but some village chiefs confided otherwise . . .).

Jeff had also taught sailing at UCLA for five years, had run the university sailing program for two years. He also raced multihulls in world championships for seventeen years and crewed larger boats as foredeck, helmsman, and tactician/navigator in open-ocean races.

Now the Cashers had settled into Marina del Rey and were living on *Sea Witch,* and Jeff had a day job, working as a solution architect for Teradata. He was actually one of Teradata's first "virtual employees." Jeff spent his workdays on *Sea Witch,* designing systems for, and troubleshooting, some of the largest computers in the world—two of them *the* largest—for major companies like Apple, Walmart, and eBay.

By the time Jeff joined Team Abby, most of *Wild Eyes* new systems had already been installed. But as an experienced circumnavigator, when Jeff looked over *Wild Eyes'* power monitoring system, he didn't like what he saw. Abby would have three ways of generating power to run her lights and instrumentation: solar panels, wind generators, and a diesel engine. Under the rules of single-handing, she would not be able to use the engine to propel her boat, only to generate power, which would then be stored in marine batteries. Solar- and wind-generated power would also funnel into *Wild Eyes'* batteries for storage.

The technician who had installed the system was a good friend of Laurence's, a man with many years of experience. On the one hand, Jeff knew he was a newcomer to the team and was reluctant to criticize a journeyman's work. On the other hand, it was his job to point out critical factors that would likely cause failure. Jeff was used to people's typical initial reaction: "He can't be right!" He was also used to people getting angry when they realized that he usually was.

In the case of *Wild Eyes,* Jeff knew that the man who had wired the power monitoring system was a capable and experienced man. But Jeff felt strongly that the man's experience did not include *Wild Eyes'* AGM batteries, which were newer on the market. Nor did he have the experience of factoring in the effects on power generation of the sun's angle at different points on the earth, or whether the batteries had sufficient storage capacity to outlast long spans of overcast or dead calm days, when no new solar or wind power was being generated.

A pretty straightforward guy, Jeff didn't have to muster much courage to voice his concerns to Laurence, who listened carefully, then invited Jeff to talk to the technician, who told Jeff that he completely disagreed. His configuration and calculations were fine, he said.

Faced with two experts with opposing opinions, Laurence did what any good project manager would do: he called in the expert of experts.

Scott Lurie, owner of Scott's Marine Services, was well known on the waterfront. He had gotten his first boat at age eleven, and even then seemed to be good at tinkering. Between the ages of sixteen and thirty, he attended U.S. Navy damage control school; crewed on tall ships and luxury yachts (once on an eighty-foot powerboat owned by David Walberg, the producer of *Roots*—guests aboard included Claire Trevor and Rock Hudson); sailed his own thirty-one-foot boat through the Panama Canal and around the Caribbean; earned his private pilot's license; learned aerobatics; attended Northrup University and became an A&P (airframe and power plant) mechanic; learned marine electrical and electronics; and earned a captain's license to operate 100-ton, 150-foot boats.

In short, if there was gear aboard a boat or an airplane that needed to be fixed, Scott Lurie could likely fix it. As a shipwright, Laurence had worked with Scott before. And when Scott looked over *Wild Eyes'* power generation setup, he agreed with Jeff.

Knowing Scott's reputation, Laurence's technician friend happily rewired the system. Scott might have done it himself, but he had just been hit by a truck while riding his bicycle. His hand was in a cast, metal rods poked out of his fingertips, and he had six titanium plates in his face. So Scott talked the technician through the process step-by-step, and Team Abby moved forward with two new members—Jeff and Scott—and no hard feelings.

CHAPTER 6

CRITICS AND "REALITY"

THOUSAND OAKS, CALIFORNIA
NOVEMBER 2009–JANUARY 2010

The refit of *Wild Eyes* was well in hand when a company named Magnetic Entertainment approached the Sunderlands about the possibility of shopping some kind of film based on Zac's and Abby's solo trips around the world. Chris Bates was a producer with Magnetic. For the proposed Sunderland project, Chris was working with a friend of his, videographer Ted Caloroso. Ted's brother had been involved in Zac's campaign on some level, and it was through Ted that Chris got in touch with the Sunderlands.

Marianne and Laurence had reason to be cautious about the film industry. Before Zac's trip, another group had approached them and pitched the idea of doing a reality show. The Sunderlands were loosely acquainted with the filmmakers through their homeschool group and trusted them. Meanwhile, the whole Sunderland family was busy prepping for Zac's campaign—too busy (and too naïve, Laurence and Marianne now admit) to have a lawyer review the "shopping agreement" that would allow the filmmakers to try and sell the concept to various networks.

They can try to shop it if they want to, Marianne remembers thinking, as she and Laurence signed the agreement. *What have we got to lose?*

A lot, as it turned out.

The business relationship ended badly because the Sunderlands, trusting the filmmakers' verbal description of the shopping agreement, failed to read the fine print, which gave away far more rights than the Sunderlands realized.

The Sunderlands then hired another production company to create a documentary using footage from the first part of Zac's trip. The company was supposed to have the editing done by the time Zac returned in July 2009. They didn't. That relationship also ended badly. The filmmakers kept the money the Sunderlands paid them to edit the documentary, but refused to return film footage to the family—even footage Zac had shot himself and footage the Sunderlands had paid travel costs for the filmmakers to obtain, such as Zac's Panama Canal passage.

Twice burned, the Sunderlands were leery of getting involved in another documentary or reality show of any kind. But Chris and Ted came across as professional, friendly, creative guys who had lots of projects in development, lots of ideas they were trying to flesh out and sell. The Sunderlands decided to let the discussion proceed and see where it went.

At first Chris and Ted suggested a show that would follow Abby's trip. But because she wasn't stopping, they decided there really wouldn't be enough material to put together any kind of show with weekly episodes. Chris and Ted talked other ideas around with their Hollywood contacts and came up with what they thought might be a workable—and salable—concept. It would be a family show that followed Abby's solo-round, worked in Zac's trip as "back-story," and also followed Zac as he prepared for his next adventure (at the time Zac was thinking of training to climb Mt. Everest). In addition, the show would delve into Laurence's business as a shipwright and Marianne's life as a home-school mom juggling seven kids, including two adventurers.

The Sunderlands liked the concept, which they saw as an inspirational, inside look at an alternative way of raising kids. Not the definitive way of raising them, just a close-up on how *one* family does it. Instead of having them educated in a cookie-cutter school system, for example, the Sunderlands followed state-approved core academic curriculum, but also encouraged each child to follow his or her own lights, to develop and explore the individual gifts God had given them. Especially important to Laurence was one underlying theme of the show: to encourage children and teens to step out into the real world, to abandon the electronic cages of Facebook, texting, and video games, and to aspire to achieve great things.

While Laurence managed the boat, Marianne managed Abby's website, blog, and other social networking sites. She kept track of interest in Abby's trip in general, and also among sailors. There were critics, of course. At first the criticism wasn't personal—mainly the same question the Sunderlands had answered when Zac put to sea: *Should a sixteen-year-old be doing this?* Their answer regarding their daughter was the same as it had been for their son: "We don't recommend it for every sixteen-year-old. But we feel Abby's ready and she's going to have the best equipment to minimize the risks."

Some bloggers were asking fair questions about the speed of preparation for Abby's trip, as well as her weather window. And their comments weren't mean-spirited.

On one site, a man calling himself CruiserJim wrote: "[N]ot ideal setting off with a bunch of newly installed stuff that's only been shaken down on a couple of quick overnight jaunts. Also, she's setting out a bit later than originally planned. Hope she's made of the same stuff as [Australian single-hander] Jessica Watson. But she set the goal to go, and she's left the dock. Fair winds, Abby."[1]

Another criticism was, why do it for a record?

Abby's dream had never been to be the youngest to single-hand around the world. But a young person who's capable beyond her years and beyond her peers is intriguing. So if she went for the record, she had a "hook" for getting a sponsorship to finance her trip. Now, in an ironic twist, some bloggers were beginning to accuse the Sunderlands of angling for a sponsorship so they could force Abby to try for the record and make themselves filthy rich in the process. This, after Marianne had first tried to use the sponsorship angle to shut down the trip.

One blogger carped, "I guess [the parents] are betting on the outcome. They'll sell the story to *Entertainment Tonight* or any other one of those useless gossip TV shows. The only way the family loses is if she doesn't make it in time to set the youngest record. If she does make it or if she dies or sinks in the attempt, the family will get paid enough to pay off the boat."[2]

When she read that, Marianne was horrified and also glad Laurence was too busy with Abby and *Wild Eyes* to spend much time reading the Internet.

What kind of a person, Marianne wondered, *thought any amount of money was worth losing a child?*

 The criticism was pretty intense. When my brother Zac did his solo-round the year before, the public and the sailing community thought sending a sixteen-year-old guy was a little crazy. But when I announced my solo-round try in 2009, it seemed like a lot of the world suffered immediate short-term memory loss. Zac had proven that my family knew what they were doing. You might think that respect would get passed along to me, but instead it was like columnists and much of the sailing community instantly forgot what my family had already done.

A lot of the criticism came from people who had never met me, and also from people who had never sailed before. Some of them did take the time to come down to the marina, talk to me, and see the work we were doing on the boat. And a lot of those people went away with changed minds. They could see that we *did* have the best experts refitting *Wild Eyes* and that my dad *did* know what he was doing. And after they talked to me, they could tell I knew what I was doing, too. The fact that so many people didn't bother to come talk to us and get first-hand information showed us that a lot of critics not only didn't know what they were talking about but also didn't care to find out.

The main criticism was that I was too young. Okay, I was a few months younger than Zac when he sailed around the world; but I was only a couple of months younger than Mike Perham, who beat Zac's record. Plus, I had grown up sailing *with* Zac, who had just completed his solo try. I had every bit as much sailing experience as he did before he set out.

Then they said, well, it's different . . . Abby's a girl. And I thought, *Wait a minute, didn't America already have this battle forty years ago?* It's not like we were talking about the NFL or professional hockey—it's *sailing.* Some of the world's most successful sailors have been women: Ellen MacArthur, Dawn Riley, and Jessica Watson, who is the same age as me and started her circumnavigation just a couple of months before I was supposed to launch.

Then, as if my age and gender were crowbars that pried open the door, the critics barged in to harp on every decision we made: I was going at the wrong time of year. *Wild Eyes* was the wrong boat. The Southern Ocean was the wrong route. (They had also criticized Zac for taking the equator route!)

The thing that drove me the craziest were the people who claimed to be able to read our minds. I just wanted to be famous, they said. That was so crazy! I was terrified doing my first interviews. I wanted to do anything *but* become famous and have that become my life. I just loved sailing.

Sadly, I began to doubt myself. Maybe I *was* too young. Maybe I *wasn't* a good enough sailor. When you read enough of that stuff, it knocks your confidence. You start to believe it. At fifteen, leading up to my sixteenth birthday in October 2009, I was at an age when I was figuring out who I was. (I still am.) There was some truth in the idea that I was immature—not in my sailing, but in my ability to emotionally handle people criticizing me. That had always been hard for me because I was shy and quiet—not the type of person to stand up for myself. All of a sudden I was having to stand up in front of all these people and say they were wrong and I was right. That was completely out of character for me.

At first I found myself trying to respond to all of it. I wanted to make everybody happy. I knew if I spoke to people personally, they'd change their minds about my level of maturity. But pretty soon I realized I'd never to be able to please everyone. And I understood that what I needed to do was focus on the task at hand, and do the very best job on the thing that I was very best at: sailing.

It was still tough to sit still for the criticism of my family, though. I got really depressed reading all this stuff trashing my mom and dad—news reports, blog comments, stuff like that. People said my dad didn't know what he was doing? *What?* He'd been a respected shipwright for twenty-five years and had just successfully sent my brother around the world!

Some critics said stuff like: "Her parents are pushing her into it because they want to make money off her." I felt like I was Alice in Wonderland and had jumped down the rabbit hole. In a world where half of all kids are children of divorce, I'd grown up in this amazing, loving family with a dream childhood full of sailing, animals, and adventures. In a world where tons of kids don't even know their fathers, I have a father who is the sole breadwinner of our household and *still* was willing to come alongside me, teach me everything he knew about the water, and pour hours and hours into helping me make my dream come true. Here I had parents who had raised me to be self-sufficient and responsible, while still supporting me 100 percent—and they were being painted as greedy, spotlight-hungry monsters!

My solo-round try was *my* decision. After just having sent Zac around the world, my parents would much rather have had me stay home. It was hard to see them criticized for something I had chosen to do.

 As the refit and Abby's training continued, the Sunderlands met several times with Chris Bates and Ted Caloroso, refining the concept for the television program a little each time. Chris seemed extremely experienced and professional to Laurence and Marianne. Ted, while a bit of a free spirit, seemed genuinely in the Sunderlands' corner. Eventually, Magnetic sold the concept to Reveille, an independently owned television and film studio with facilities on the Universal Studios lot. Reveille had many successful shows to its credit, including major sitcoms like *The Office, Ugly Betty*, and reality/ competition shows like *Nashville Star* and *The Biggest Loser*.

From what the Sunderlands could learn, everybody in Hollywood knew and respected Reveille. For Laurence and Marianne, just regular folks going about the business of raising their kids, to have affiliated with such a credible company was an amazing thing.

The next step was for Magnetic to put together what's known in the entertainment industry as a "sizzle reel," a fast-moving video showcase meant to grab network executives' attention and sell them on a show's concept. Ted, the videographer, shot footage in a number of places: the Sunderland home as Marianne dealt with the kids; the refit of *Wild Eyes* underway at Marina del Rey; Abby on her sea trials from a chase boat; and Zac on his boat, *Intrepid*.

As the proposed show took shape, the Sunderlands felt an entirely different vibe from Chris and Ted than they had from the filmmakers who'd burned them on Zac's documentary. Ted was very cheery and upbeat, very accommodating when he was around the Sunderland children. The Sunderlands grew to like Ted so much that Laurence arranged for him to stay aboard one of his client's boats at Marina del Rey. The seventy-foot luxury yacht was tied up just a few docks away from *Wild Eyes*. It seemed to be a perfect arrangement. Ted would have a place to store all his video equipment and would be able to get to *Wild Eyes* quickly in order to film major milestones during the refit.

Late one afternoon in December, Marianne brought the whole Sunderland clan down to the marina to take a look at the progress on Abby's boat. She didn't bring all the kids down often because *Wild Eyes* was small, dock space was limited, and it was tough keeping all the little ones rounded up. When she arrived, Marianne learned that Laurence had a few loose ends to tie up. The sun had set already and the air was getting a bit chilly. Marianne knew that they'd be waiting for a bit.

"Jessie, why don't you take Liddy, Katherine, and Ben down to the boat where Ted is staying?" Marianne said. "That way you can stay warm while we wait for Daddy to finish up."

Even at eleven, Jessie was a levelheaded caretaker of her younger brother and sisters. With seven kids, that's just the way things worked in the Sunderland home—the big kids helped out with the little ones. And even more than her older sister, Abby, Jessie seemed already to have a budding maternal streak. She liked to be given responsibility.

"Okay, Mom," she said, and headed off down the dock, ushering her charges like a mama duck.

Just before Jessie and her siblings reached Ted's borrowed yacht, they met him walking up the dock in their direction. Jessie remembers that Ted's eyes narrowed when he saw the kids and that his lips formed a thin line.

The look on Ted's face surprised Jessie. *He looks like he doesn't even like us*, she thought. Whenever Jessie had been in his presence while her parents were around, Ted was friendly and fun. Now he was completely different.

It was almost dark. A little nervous, Jessie looked up at Ted. "My mom told us to come down here to your boat and wait until my dad finishes up on Abby's boat."

Ted frowned, Jessie remembers. "Well, I just cleaned the upstairs, so make sure you all stay downstairs," he said. Then he walked off down the dock.

A little while later, Marianne and Laurence walked down from *Wild Eyes* and boarded the yacht to retrieve their kids. When Jessie brought her siblings upstairs, she heard Ted talking with her parents. And when Ted turned his eyes on the kids, he turned on his smile.

That's weird, Jessie thought. *Now he's Mr. Happy again, part of the team.*

The next night over dinner at the Sunderland home, Jessie told Laurence and Marianne about her encounter with Ted the previous evening. No, she didn't think Ted had just been having a bad day, she said. "He's putting on an act. He's not our friend."

Jessie wasn't the histrionic type, so her story got the Sunderlands' attention. *Had something changed with Ted?* they wondered. *Or was there something about him that they'd missed all along?*

In any case, Laurence and Marianne decided to be careful.

 Just as the refit was winding up, Abby's campaign acquired a last-minute sponsor. It was a tri-sponsorship, actually, with Krikorian Premier Theaters, SS AquaFriends, and Lucky Cat TV all pitching in critically needed funds. There probably aren't enough adjectives to describe Abby's and her family's gratitude because, as Laurence put it, "The refit was a very expensive part of the operation. Very, very, very expensive." The generous eleventh-hour sponsorship would provide critical support as Abby's journey unfolded.

By the end of December, *Wild Eyes* was ready for her shakedown cruises. A shakedown cruise is a period of operational testing for a boat, and also a time when the crew gets familiar with a new vessel. Abby did four such sails, also called "sea trials." The first two were brief trips with rigger and veteran single-hander Alan Blunt, and UK-Halsey sailmaker Oliver McCain. During these sails, Alan and Oliver checked the fit and operation of the sails, and Abby's ability to handle them. Both Abby and the sails worked beautifully.

On January 12, Abby did a hundred-mile solo overnight trip through the Channel Islands. The winds were light for a time, then picked up but died down again. This was a good opportunity for her to practice reefing with the new sails and rigging. That night, as she passed Santa Barbara Island, Abby's autopilots failed, revealing a system that needed more work.

Laurence used Abby's fourth sea trial as a way to double-check his own thinking. Was his daughter really as expert a sailor as he thought she was? Or was he just a proud papa? Worse, had the crush and excitement of the whole project cursed him with tunnel vision?

Laurence had already told Abby that the chances of her completing her trip nonstop were about fifty/fifty, strictly because of the high probability of equipment failure on any such attempt. But Laurence didn't want to tip the percentages into the negative column with any shortsightedness on his own part. That's why he turned to Alan Blunt.

Laurence and Alan had raced together in 1995 on the *New Zealand Endeavor*, one of the most famous Maxi-class yachts in the world. Alan, a world-class sailor, had sailed in the Southern Ocean and worked and raced on boats for more than thirty years. He had been in several Sidney to Hobart races and had even survived a cyclone at sea. Laurence greatly respected Alan's opinion and knew that if he asked Alan his opinion of Abby's sailing abilities, Alan wouldn't mince words.

On January 17, Abby and Alan sailed a hundred miles overnight in fairly mild conditions around Santa Catalina Island. When they returned the next morning, Laurence pulled Alan aside at the dock.

After Alan downloaded a general assessment of *Wild Eyes*' readiness, Laurence asked, "What do you think of Abby's sailing abilities?"

"I've got no problem with her sailing ability," Alan said. "She'll be just fine."

By this time, bloggers had begun carping that Abby would be sailing an untested boat into treacherous conditions. Others said Abby didn't have enough time aboard *Wild Eyes* before taking her around the world. But between the sail down the Eastern Seaboard, the trip up from Ensenada, and her sea trials, Abby had sailed around fifteen hundred miles on *Wild Eyes* by the time she launched her campaign.

As the launch date neared, work on the boat, and in particular on the autopilots and the Automatic Identification System (AIS) (a collision-avoidance system to keep *Wild Eyes* clear of other boats), continued at a furious pace. Abby's voyage depended heavily on a weather window that Commanders' Weather had determined would get her safely through the Southern Ocean. However, her trip was not, as some critics charged, up against a sponsorship deadline. It was true that since the Sunderlands had already spent a hefty portion of the sponsorship money on the refit, it was imperative that Abby sail. But the major sponsor had put Laurence squarely in charge of the date. When the original December launch date was delayed due to refit issues, Laurence called the Shoe City representative who had been handling the sponsorship details. "We're going to have a delay here," Laurence told him. "I wanted to let you know that and make sure it's okay."

"We don't care when Abby sets sail," the Shoe City rep said. "We just want to make sure that everything is right, and the boat is safe. When it's right, have her go."

On January 22, the day before Abby was scheduled to depart, Laurence was standing at the top of the dock where *Wild Eyes* was berthed. Unseasonable rains had been pounding Southern California and hampering work on the boat. The storms had moved on, but the air hung damp and cool, and a thick cloud layer stretched across the marina like a low, gray blanket.

From where he was standing, Laurence could see at least a dozen workers swarming on and around the boat, and he thought for perhaps the hundredth time about the incredible commitment of the people involved in Abby's trip. To Laurence, their unity, and even the speed of resolution during technical disagreements, was nothing short of amazing. It was as though the team had gelled into a single mind working toward a single goal: getting Abigail to sea.

As he was reflecting on these things, Laurence saw Jeff Casher step off *Wild Eyes* and walk up to meet him. As was his style, Jeff got right to the point. "Laurence, it still seems like there's too much to be done before she is supposed to leave."

Jeff said he was concerned because some of Abby's technical systems hadn't been tested under realistic conditions at sea. Part of this was because of the crush of the refit timeline, and part because of workdays lost due to bad weather.

Laurence agreed that things aboard *Wild Eyes* weren't perfect. There were still some issues with the AIS and autopilots, for example. "You know, we've had a few letdowns and setbacks, and I would've liked things to be different," Laurence said. "Tomorrow, if the boat is good to go, Abby will go. If it's not, she won't. And if she needs to pull in, we'll pull her in."

It might be, Laurence told Jeff, that Abigail's first leg to Cape Horn would turn out to be a sea trial to Cabo.

The truth about any nonstop circumnavigation attempt is that it is really a series of "legs" that the crew and support team hope will ultimately form a circle around the globe, unbroken by stops. But contingency ports are always plotted out along the route. And when problems arise, the shore team researches available berthing and repair facilities at various possible landing points. The hope, of course, is that the crew won't have to put in. But if they do, plans are already in motion.

The conversation with Laurence put Jeff at ease. The fact was, *Wild Eyes* was completely worthy to sail to Cabo without any risk or danger. Even if every one of Abby's technical systems failed, she could hand steer to Cabo if she had to. It's what sailors have done for centuries: get from point A to point B using wind, sails, and a tiller. Jeff could see that Laurence wasn't hell-bent on a nonstop. Rather, he had accepted that under the circumstances, *Wild Eyes* was as good as she was going to get, and that if Abby had to stop for repairs, she had to stop for repairs. Laurence wasn't going to put his daughter's life at risk for a record.

CHAPTER 7

FAIR WINDS AND FOLLOWING SEAS

MARINA DEL REY, CALIFORNIA
JANUARY 2010

 My official launch was set for January 23, 2010. But for days the skies had been dumping buckets on Marina del Rey and barometric pressures had fallen to record lows. The weather was not just unusual; it was bizarre. There was even a tornado that touched down in Long Beach, flipping a catamaran in its berth. Because of the crazy rain, our refit schedule was as muddied up as the yacht club lawn. Issues with the autopilots and the AIS were giving the technicians so much trouble that there was a chance I might not be able to leave on time.

The night before I was supposed to launch, my dad and I stayed down at the marina until like one in the morning, but the guys kept working the problems until nearly sunrise. Several guys from my team told me to expect the next day to be a blur that I would barely remember. "Kind of like the day you get married," one of them said.

I was thinking, *Great. Since I'm only sixteen, I have no idea what you mean. But at least I'll know what to expect on my wedding day!*

Dad and I drove home to Thousand Oaks and tried to get some sleep. I was too wiped out to feel much of anything except exhaustion. I had slept maybe three hours when Dad got up and called the techs, who were still down at the marina.

Yes, they said, the autopilots and AIS were up and running. My departure was a go!

As I prepared to leave my house, the mixture of physical and emotional stuff going on inside me was so crazy that my stomach felt like a blender somebody had switched on high. I was so happy, nervous, excited, and anxious all at the same time, and an adrenaline buzz was getting me past my short night's sleep. On the other hand, I'd had a cold for a few days, so I couldn't breathe through my nose, which stunk because I knew I would be giving a press conference at the Del Rey Yacht Club that morning before I set sail. I was nervous enough about that without having to worry about sounding like I had a clothespin clipped on my nose.

Dad and I got in the car to head back to the marina; Mom would be driving down with my brothers and sisters in a couple of hours. As we backed out of the driveway, I looked at my house. I had never missed it much before when I was at sea. But then again, I was usually at sea with at least one person from my family. So it wasn't just a house I was leaving this time. It was my whole family. It was kind of surreal to think that I wouldn't see them again for the better part of a year.

I was usually the quiet one while Dad chatted away about this and that. But we were both quiet on the way to Marina del Rey, thinking about everything that was about to happen. During the night, the team had moved *Wild Eyes* from the marina to the Del Rey Yacht Club, my official launch point. Our first stop was to see the boat and put some last minute supplies aboard, like a pillow and a stuffed doggie, to keep me company.

From there, we walked up to the main room at the yacht club, where the press conference was already forming up. When we walked in, I was amazed at the number of people there—club members, well-wishers, curious people, and lots and lots of press. I was pretty much terrified. I mean literally shaking, which is why it cracked me up when I later read the critics who said I was only doing this whole thing to get attention.

By that time Mom, Zac, and the rest of my siblings had arrived. Sherry Barone, a yacht club board member, had been kind enough to organize my departure from the club. Nate 'n Al, a local Thousand Oaks deli, had donated coffee, juice, and bagels. There was a big table at the front of the room and I took a seat at the center. Dad, Mom, and Zac were up there with me. I was supposed to start off by giving a statement, but when I started talking, the crowded room swelled in my imagination to the size of a stadium, making me that much more terrified. To this day, I don't remember much of what I said. I know I thanked our sponsors and my team for all their support. I also remember hoping that I wasn't saying anything stupid.

Then we all sat up front and took questions from reporters and the crowd. There were a lot of doom-and-gloom questions: What if this breaks down? What if that breaks down? What if you get a wave that's too big? What if you die?

"The boat's set up as well as it can be," I said. "Part of being mentally prepared is knowing there are going to be great times out there—and there are probably going to be times when I wish I wasn't there."

A lot of people also asked technical questions. How much fuel do you carry? How much water? How many months' worth of food?

I remember one specific question. Someone, I think it was a reporter, asked me, "What's the longest amount of time you've been at sea alone?"

The answer was: twenty-four hours. I hated answering that question because it made me look like I couldn't possibly know what I was doing. There was no way out of it, so I just told the truth. I had learned that with reporters, the bolder you are, the better things go. It's almost like they can smell weakness. They're not usually out and out rude, but I had talked to some reporters who seemed sort of amused, smiling as they condescended to me. It was almost like because I was only sixteen, they thought I didn't know what attitude they were projecting. I didn't know which was worse—the reporters who I *knew* weren't going to write something very nice, or the ones who were nice to my face, then wrote terrible things.

During the whole press conference, my stomach churned. I must've done okay, though, because one reporter later wrote that I seemed calmer than some of the adults around me. And my mom told me that I appeared really low-key, answering all the questions about my boat and my trip as easily as if I was discussing a sale at the mall. (Which actually would've been harder for me to discuss, now that I think about it.)

Some of my best friends were at the conference, and at the very end, my friend Kasey Nash stood up and asked everyone to bow their heads. Then she prayed aloud for my voyage and safe return.

 Though the Del Rey Yacht Club hosted Abby's press conference, many club members were opposed to her trip. Some, along with others in the sailing community, had made their opinions known, both verbally and in yachting and sailing publications. This was long before the mainstream press started weighing in on Abby's solo try.

The criticism from the boating community didn't bother Laurence as much as it perplexed him. He was amazed that so many people felt it was their right to deliver judgments based on nothing more than a sliver of the whole picture. These people weren't there at the beginning of Abigail's life, Laurence thought. They didn't raise her on boats. They weren't there when Abigail cruised on the Aleutian for three years.

They didn't know her temperament or how she dealt with adversity. To Laurence, the uninformed criticism was nothing short of bizarre.

One thing was certain: a good number of yachters weren't in his corner. Laurence was just a blue-collar guy from the marina, elbow deep in engines, a screwdriver in his hand. He was well aware that the Sunderland family had crashed the party with Zac's solo-round success. Because of that rare achievement—and not their own wealth or social status—the family enjoyed memberships at a number of yacht clubs, and they did like the social aspects. But Laurence did not think that having the money to buy a yacht and sail (usually with a hired crew) to Catalina three or four times a year qualified people to judge either his parenting or his marine expertise. Some of those critics were among the questioners at the press conference, and Laurence didn't try to impress them. "You know the bottom line is, every kid will learn to drive. Do we stop them from driving because they might have an accident? We're trying to protect the young so much that we stifle their development. This was years in preparation and years of work, and I'm very excited for Abigail."

As the questioning went on, Laurence sensed the mood change in the room. As he and Abby answered question after question, it seemed to allay many people's concerns. Del Rey Yacht Club member Roberta Feldman later told a reporter that Abby's conduct at the press conference changed her mind.

"I had my doubts before," she said. "But she's very sophisticated for sixteen years old. I have great confidence in her now."[1]

Several others came up to Laurence and Marianne at separate times and said they felt differently after hearing Abby speak.

"I was totally against this," one club member told Laurence. "But I can see now that you are so well prepared. You've got all your *i*'s dotted and your *t*'s crossed."

Some people told Laurence and Marianne they'd been emotionally moved by the things Abby had said. Before, they had been skeptics;

now they understood that Abby had spent her life on the ocean, and that the ocean was her life.

The press conference completed, Sandra and Jason, from Abby's cosponsor SS Aquafriends, presented Abby, Zac, Marianne, and Laurence with genuine leis made of Hawaiian flowers and greenery. Then the whole menagerie headed down to the dock where some members of Team Abby were still doing last-minute prep on the boat. Already the dock was crowded with hundreds of friends, well-wishers, and perhaps a skeptic (or ten). Now, followed by reporters and television cameras, the Sunderlands inched their way through the throng to where *Wild Eyes*, Abby's home for the next several months, was tied up and waiting for her.

Abby and Laurence stepped aboard and began checking over the vessel one last time. Then Abby stepped off the boat and back onto the dock.

"What are you doing?" Marianne asked her.

Abby grinned. "Enjoying the concrete while I've still got it."

 I hadn't really meant for anyone except Mom to hear that concrete comment, but some in the crowd closest to us got a good laugh out of it. I heard later that some reporters said I looked calm and efficient, but with everyone watching my every move, I was *soooo* nervous! The hectic preparations the previous evening, my short night's sleep, the last-minute decision that the sail was a go, the agony of the press conference, and being the total center of attention— it rattled my nerves.

As I pulled away from the dock, I remembered what my team said the night before about this day being like my wedding day, and thought, *If this is what getting married is like, maybe I'll stay single!*

I did a pretty good job of looking cool on the outside. But even from a distance, my rigger, Alan Blunt, noticed that I seemed a little slow in preparing to raise the mainsail. He motored up beside *Wild Eyes* in a dinghy and called me over to the side. "You're a good girl, Abby. Forget about the cameras, and the people and the reporters and all that," Alan said, looking up at me. "You can do this. So get going and get the mainsail up."

Alan's words helped snap me out of the publicity blur back into the reason I was there: to get *Wild Eyes* under way.

 To see Abby off, Laurence had use of a seventy-foot yacht. Six Sunderlands—Laurence, Marianne, Jessica, Lydia, Katherine, and Ben—climbed aboard, along with Marianne's mother and Abby's friends Christina, Amber, Audrey, and Kasey; representatives from Abby's sponsors; and a select group of reporters.

At 10:57 Pacific Time, Abby officially got underway. After the week of stormy weather, she set sail under sunny skies, on a glassy sea with a big swell running. Along with Laurence's yacht, several police and fire boats motored out to send Abby off, and the Sunderlands could see fire engines lined up along the walkway to the breakwater, hailing her as she sailed by.

With her full sail up, ghosting along the glistening swells, Laurence thought *Wild Eyes* looked majestic. He and Marianne wrestled with conflicting emotions. They were excited to see Abby launch her dream, but still nervous and already looking forward to that first satellite phone call. Then, both were moved nearly to tears when they saw Zac and Toby come sailing up alongside Abby in Zac's boat, *Intrepid*. He had sailed around the world on that boat, coming full circle in a very literal sense. Now the Sunderlands were watching their oldest daughter set off on the same quest with her older brother cheering her on.

The Sunderlands had planned to motor only a mile or so out, but Laurence's heartstrings kept pulling him along. Later that night, they revealed to each other that they'd been sharing the same thought: *Let's not turn back. Let's just sail around the world with her.*

Laurence guided the powerboat up and down the big swells, which shone back at him like mirrors. Sometimes *Wild Eyes'* sails would dip down in a trough and he would lose sight of Abby completely. He thought this might be what it's like when you see a young lady leave home and move out on her own. Having spent so much of Abby's life with her on the water, it was like that for Laurence—as if he were sending his daughter out into the world for the first time.

 With all the excitement and festivities of my send-off, I would've loved to sail away with *Wild Eyes'* sails full of wind. Instead, when I turned off my engine, the wind didn't cooperate, so I made my grand departure at about . . . oh, two knots. Looking back at the dock, I saw tons of people. Up close, I hadn't been able to tell how many people had come to see me off. Now at a distance, I was humbled and amazed.

My family and some friends followed me out on a big powerboat, and there were a bunch of other sailboats kind of escorting me out. For a while, the big yacht my dad was driving was close enough that I could see my friends Christine, Audrey, Kasey, and Amber sitting on the bow and hear them yelling to me.

"Have fun!"

"Be careful!"

"We'll go to Starbucks when you get back!"

When my little flotilla of boats reached El Segundo, one of my phones rang. It was my dad and he sounded, I don't know, a little more emotional than usual. "Abby, I've got a nice dinner waiting for you at home," he said. "It's going to be ready in about seven months' time. Make sure you're not late for dinner."

CHAPTER 8

DOLPHINS AND SUNSETS

**MARINA DEL REY TO CABO
JANUARY 2010**

 No land anywhere, water all around, the deep blue of sapphires. Clouds layered on the horizon, dyed hot pink and scarlet, beams of light breaking through to turn the water gold. It's a whole different feeling watching the sunset alone, out in the middle of the ocean—the sun a huge globe of fire, rolling out light like a shimmering carpet. It was so different from watching the sunset from land, where you're safe and warm and dry. It's like the difference between looking at a picture of a place and being in that place. Sitting on *Wild Eyes'* deck drenched in golden light, I felt I could hold up my hand and touch the sun.

The first few days at sea were a steep learning curve—not learning how to sail, but learning when to eat and sleep while still keeping *Wild Eyes* shipshape and underway. During the first three days, I found that

I slept as much during the day as at night because keeping up with the boat required being up at all hours.

I learned that the work was a good thing. Staying busy helped me get used to life alone on the water. When you come from a family where there are *nine* people in the house nearly all the time, it's a little disconcerting to have the world fall suddenly silent. That didn't mean I didn't like it—I loved it. But it was still a little weird.

Sailing south under light winds, I felt like *Wild Eyes* was *crawling*. I could've made better time in a rowboat! I felt like a racehorse at the starting gate. I knew what *Wild Eyes* could do and I kept wishing God would cooperate and fill her sails!

On the evening of the first day, I passed Catalina Island. From there, I turned due south and by the afternoon of January 24, God smiled on me with twelve-knot winds. I made twenty-four miles in three hours, passed out of American waters and even made it south of Ensenada, Mexico, by evening.

On my way south I had two kinds of visitors: squids and dolphins. Sometimes a few dolphins would come and splash around my bow. I felt like they were welcoming me to the Pacific Ocean. Other times *Wild Eyes* would draw a whole pod and I would be sailing along amidst two dozen or more dolphins, arcing through the water, surfing in my wake. I could see them dart under the boat. They had such a happy look about them, they made me smile. I remember thinking that I had never seen an unhappy dolphin. Do dolphins have bad days? I don't think so.

When the dolphins came at night, they left trails in phosphorescent green and when they jumped out of the water, the glowing green foam arced up with them and splashed down again.

The squid weren't nearly as much fun. On my second day at sea, I climbed up in the cockpit and saw a squid sitting there looking up at me. He was only about three inches long. At first I wondered how in the world he'd gotten into my boat, since I'd never heard of flying squid. I decided he must have surfed in on a breaking wave. Maybe he was lonely and happy to have company. Or was it a girl squid? I didn't know. But I did know I don't much like squid. Using just my forefinger and thumb and making as little skin contact as possible, I plucked him/her up by a tentacle and flung him/her overboard.

Maybe that was a mistake. The next morning, I found a whole bunch of squid up on deck, their squishy bodies tucked into weird corners, lurking in the middle of coiled lines. I figured the first squid I threw back must have dove down and invited his friends. ("Hey, everybody! There's a boat up there! Let's party!") After that, I spent every morning cleaning the squid off *Wild Eyes'* deck. Maybe I should've just let the first little guy stay aboard.

During the first week, between managing my power consumption, keeping my sails trimmed, and making sure *Wild Eyes* stayed shipshape, I also tried to keep up with my blog. After my third day out, I didn't see anyone—no boats, no ships, nobody but squid and dolphin. So it was fun to be in contact with people even though I was way out in the Pacific.

A lot of commenters on my blog asked what I'd been eating. Here's how I answered:

For the first few days, I didn't eat much of anything. My stomach just couldn't handle it.

That surprised me some. I had grown up on the water. I'd been sailing small boats nearly all my life and in rough seas. But there was something about the deep water in a small boat that was different.

After a few days, though, my stomach got its sea legs and I started eating the fresh food that I'd packed for the first week. Kristy Morrell, a registered dietician who also works as the sports dietician for the athletic programs at the University of Southern California, had volunteered to help me create a nutritional plan for my trip. We talked for a long time about what conditions I'd be living under and how that would affect my nutritional needs. A solo-round campaign has some similarities to a space flight. You're working with limited storage space, limited weight capacity, and little ability to preserve fresh food items. For those reasons, I ended up with quite a bit of dehydrated food, the kind astronauts and serious mountain climbers eat. My food was packed in watertight bags, one for each week of my journey. My mom was the best: she was really careful to pack a little bit of chocolate in each week's food bag. Because, you know, when you're feeling a little down, chocolate is good medicine. (Although the team doctor, David Lowenberg, head of the ER at Stanford University hospital, might not agree!)

Kristy also recommended power snacks like dried fruit, nuts, protein bars, and beef jerky. That was a good thing because keeping up the boat required being up at all hours of the day and night. There was so much to do, with troubleshooting little problems, monitoring my power usage, and checking to see that my radar and other equipment were running and accurate. I spent most of my time either outside in the cockpit or down below at my chart desk. In between all the maintenance, I'd grab a little sleep here and there, but after a few days, catnaps weren't enough. I remembered Zac's advice about how important it was to get quality sleep. So on my fourth night out, I unlatched my bed from the bulkhead, pulled it down, and actually got a good night's sleep.

On my fifth day out, January 27, conditions were sunny and perfect. I was making good speed, surfing down the wave fronts at about seven knots. I didn't yell, "Yaaa-hooo!" or anything, but it was that much fun!

Unfortunately I didn't know how much wind I had because my gauges had decided to stop working. And the next day, my wind was gone. Since there was no sun either, my batteries were draining fast. That meant I would soon have no power for the autopilots and would have to hand steer for a while until my wind generators and solar panels could generate and store up more.

But I wasn't to that point yet and there wasn't much to do that day in terms of maintenance, so I actually considered pulling out my schoolbooks. Then I decided that was a nasty thought. Instead, I called home and discussed my power generation issues with my team.

Since leaving Marina del Rey, I had been keeping a close eye on my power consumption, testing different ways to manage it, doing whatever I could to make it work. The super-light winds I'd had most of the way down the Baja Peninsula had revealed a problem: I was just not able to make enough power with my solar panels and wind generators to keep up with all my energy needs. Because of the low winds, I'd had to run my alternators quite a bit, and we found we hadn't budgeted enough fuel to keep up with that demand.

On January 30, I announced on my blog that I would be pulling into Cabo. The team would meet me down there. Dad, Scott, and Jeff had decided to increase my storage capacity by adding two big marine batteries. They would also be putting several additional jury cans of fuel aboard *Wild Eyes* as added insurance, in case I ran into long patches of light winds—in the Doldrums, for example, an area near the equator where dead calm days are common.

 On January 23, Bill Bennett was at his Los Angeles home watching the evening news when a story aired about a young girl who had just set sail from Marina del Rey on a solo voyage around the world.

Wow, Bill thought. *That's courageous.*

A cinematographer and private pilot, Bill had always been inspired watching young people striving to do significant things. Right on the spot, he Googled "Abby Sunderland," found her blog, and began to follow her trip. Every two or three days, Bill checked in on Abby's progress down the coast of California, on her way to Cape Horn. Then on January 30, he noticed an announcement on her blog: Abby was putting in at Cabo San Lucas, Mexico, because of problems with power generation and her wind indicators.

Instantly an idea struck Bill. He had worked all over the world as a cinematographer in developed nations of Europe and the Orient and also in remote, third world countries in Africa. And he had been on more than one million-dollar-a-day production that came to a grinding halt for lack of a one-dollar part that was readily available almost anywhere except where the production location was. Bill thought there was a pretty good chance that Team Abby might encounter just that type of problem in Cabo. As the owner of a private plane, he decided he was in a position to help.

It'll be an adventure, he thought. *And I'm always up for an adventure.*

Bill pulled up Abby's website and sent an e-mail in the blind to the Sunderlands:

FIRST NAME: BILL
LAST NAME: BENNETT

I READ ON ABBY'S BLOG THAT SHE IS GOING TO HAVE TO PUT INTO CABO TO MAKE ADJUSTMENTS AND REPAIRS, THEN RE-START FROM THERE. KNOWING HOW THESE THINGS GO, MORE THAN LIKELY THERE WILL BE ONE OR TWO PARTS THE TEAM WILL DISCOVER THEY NEED, YET MIGHT ONLY BE AVAILABLE IN LOS ANGELES OR SAN DIEGO. I OWN A BONANZA A36 AIRPLANE. I AM VOLUNTEERING MY TIME AND THE AIRCRAFT TO FLY ANY LAST MINUTE PARTS AND PIECES DOWN TO CABO IF YOU NEED IT. MY PLANE CAN MAKE CABO FROM BURBANK, WHERE IT IS BASED, IN ABOUT 5.5 HOURS, NON-STOP. I COULD STOP IN SAN DIEGO TO GET THE PARTS ALONG THE WAY IF NECESSARY. LET ME KNOW IF I CAN HELP OUT. I WOULD BE GLAD TO DO IT.

BILL BENNETT, CINEMATOGRAPHER.

At the very end of the message, he included the number to his personal cell phone. Two hours later, it rang.

"Hello, this is Laurence Sunderland speaking," said an affable-sounding man with an Australian accent. "Are you the airplane pilot?"

At first Bill was a bit confused—he hadn't been expecting somebody with an Aussie accent. The caller then clarified, "I'm Laurence Sunderland, Abigail Sunderland's father. You wrote the e-mail offering to fly parts down to Cabo San Lucas to help Abby's boat?"

"Okay, yes, that was me," Bill said.

"Well, here's the situation," Laurence said. "I've got these two big marine batteries. They're about twenty-four by sixteen by ten inches and each one weighs about 130 pounds. The air freight companies and airlines won't touch them because they're very heavy gel cell batteries and are considered very hazardous cargo. Can you carry them in your airplane?"

The request was direct . . . and a bit different from what Bill had been expecting. What Laurence was describing was a bit of a heavy load for a light plane. Bill did some quick mental calculations: His Bonanza A36 could carry six passengers. The batteries Laurence mentioned each weighed about as much as an average person, so if Bill removed two of the Bonanza's seats and strapped the batteries in at those spots, that would take care of weight-and-balance considerations.

"Yes," Bill said after a few moments. "I can do that!"

Abby was scheduled to put in at Cabo on Tuesday, February 2, but when Bill checked the weather forecast, he saw that a sizable storm was heading for the Baja Peninsula. To beat the storm, Bill told Laurence they would need to take off as early as possible on Monday. The two men agreed to meet at the Santa Monica airport on Monday at 9:00 a.m.

"Perfect," Laurence said. "I'll be picking up the batteries at a couple of marine supply stores on my way down."

"Will you be going by West Marine?" Bill asked, naming a particular store.

"Yes."

"Okay, while you're there, could you please pick up a portable hand-held 406 Megahertz personal locator beacon?"

A personal locator beacon (PLB) is an emergency signaling system. About six months prior, the world search-and-rescue (SAR) community had announced that it would no longer be monitoring 121.5, a VHF frequency that had for decades been a standard emergency, or "guard," channel within the SAR system worldwide. Bill's Bonanza was still equipped with the VHF locator beacon because he had been waiting for the debut of a new piece of equipment that integrated both the new UHF frequency and a global positioning system. But with two days notice before the Cabo flight, there would be no time to get that gear installed, even if Bill had had the parts already sitting in a hangar.

Bill had flown down the Baja Peninsula before. He knew that not only were there no air traffic controllers monitoring the long, isolated chunk of wilderness that stretched south of Tijuana, but that in many places there was practically no civilization at all. Knowing he would be responsible for Laurence's life as well as his own, Bill wanted to have the newer UHF signaling system aboard, just in case some emergency caused him to have to put the plane down in Baja's infamously remote terrain.

"Okay . . ." Laurence said. "I can pick up a PLB."

Bill didn't know at the time that Laurence was thinking, *Is it a good sign that this pilot, who volunteered from out of nowhere, has asked me to buy a piece of equipment that's usually activated only when a plane's about to crash?*

 As Scott Lurie drove his work van toward the Santa Monica airport with the batteries, some tools, and the new UHF beacon in tow, Laurence sat in the passenger seat thinking: *This*

guy, Bill, sounded like an older man on the phone. I wonder if his eyesight's bad? I wonder how well his plane is kept up? Maybe that's why he wants the PLB! What am I getting myself into?

After getting the batteries cleared at the gate to the airfield, Scott guided the van to the ramp where the Bonanza was parked. As they approached, Laurence sized up Bill. He was a big guy, a bit older than himself. Tall, head shaved bald, fit looking.

The plane also seems to be in good shape, Laurence thought, then laughed at himself. *Not that I know anything about planes.*

Scott and Laurence got out of the van. Handshakes and introductions all around. Bill had said he wanted to take off ASAP to beat the southern Baja storm, so the three men wasted no time loading the batteries and a healthy array of tools into the Bonanza. Bill checked his weight-and-balance charts to be sure the cargo weight was distributed properly and buttoned up the plane. Scott said his goodbyes, then Bill and Laurence climbed into the cockpit.

"You ready?" Bill said from the left seat.

"I'm ready," Laurence said. Then he saw Bill pick up some kind of manual and begin reading it as he flipped switches and turned dials.

You've got to be kidding me! Laurence thought. *He's reading a bloody how-to manual! What is this, his second day on the job?*

Laurence's brain raced as Bill continued to refer to his little manual, then flip a switch, refer again, turn a dial.

Well, I'll just watch him and see what he does, Laurence thought. *That way, if he has a heart attack or something, I'll be able to fly the plane. How difficult could it be?*

In fact, it was very difficult: Bill was an instrument- and multi-engine-rated commercial pilot with more than twenty-two hundred flight hours. He had flown everything from single-engine Cessnas to a DC-3. He was an also an expert hang glider—he had once surfed thermals at 16,500 feet near Mt. Whitney—who was probably as qualified to land a plane with total engine failure as almost anyone except Sully Sullenberger of Hudson River fame.

But Laurence, who had never been in the cockpit of a light plane when the pilot went through the preflight checklist, mistook Bill's meticulous professionalism for a novice's reliance on a "How to Fly an Airplane" manual. Months later, after the two men had become fast friends, they had a good laugh when Laurence told Bill what he'd been thinking—and that the longer he watched Bill perform the complex series of preflight procedures, the more Laurence decided his situation was hopeless.

If this guy can't fly this plane, he thought at the time, *I'm a goner*.

The flight down the Baja peninsula took Bill and Laurence over rugged mountains, sun-bleached dry washes, and hundreds of miles with no signs of civilization at all, not even a dirt road. On a flight over the United States, hours in the cockpit would've been filled with air traffic radio chatter. But once the Bonanza buzzed south of the Tijuana terminal control area, the only people Bill and Laurence had to talk to were each other. So for the next five hours, they got acquainted.

"I've spent my entire career working in the film business," Bill said. He explained that he had been mentored by a brilliant director/cameraman named Ron Dexter, and had developed that experience into a career in television commercials—everything from iconic McDonald's restaurant ads to Super Bowl commercials. About six years earlier, he had been invited to join the American Society of Cinematographers, an honorary, by-invitation-only society that's only had 650 members since 1919. As a person whose entire career had been launched by a faithful mentor, Bill had always felt that he should "pay it forward" and help other young people pursue their dreams.

Laurence told Bill about his upbringing on the water, his work as a shipwright, the Sunderlands' cruising years, and Abby's dream to sail around the world since the age of thirteen. The two men talked a lot about Abby, because Bill had not yet met her. He had done a little sailing on Sunfish and catamarans and was fascinated by her desire and drive to take on this extraordinary challenge.

At one point, Bill said, "You know, when I started reading Abby's blog, I learned about Jessica Watson, and began to follow her trip, too."

Jessica was the sixteen-year-old Australian girl who had set the same goal for herself as Abby. She was sailing a thirty-four-foot Sparkman & Stephens and was already about three months into her campaign when Abby put to sea.

"I've noticed a common thread on Jessica's blog," Bill said. "She's either been coached by someone or maybe she's just naturally this way, but she seems very determined to keep a positive attitude throughout her trip. In every blog entry and every video she has posted on her site, she uses that phrase, 'positive mental attitude,' and I think that's very important."

Isolation of any kind, Bill had observed, can lead to an insidious kind of depression. At least when you're around other people, they can say, "Hey, you seem kind of down. Let's go out and get some ice cream," or whatever. But when you're alone, there's no one else to help you identify your condition—and no one to help you head it off before it spirals out of control.

"You're absolutely right and I've spoken with her about that very thing," Laurence said. "I call it 'stinkin' thinkin'."

"Abby's going to be by herself for six to seven months," Bill said. "How is she going to maintain a positive mental attitude?"

At that moment, Laurence turned to Bill and smiled. "Well, maybe you could talk to her about it."

"But I don't even know her," Bill said, taken aback. "You're her father. You should talk to her."

Laurence chuckled. "No, you don't understand. She's a teenager. She doesn't listen to me."

Bill, who doesn't have children, had heard parents say this before. But he had never heard it expressed so succinctly about something as vital as this.

Laurence, though, the father of both a sixteen-year-old and an eighteen-year-old whom he'd just sent around the world, had actually boiled it down to a mathematical formula: After kids turn fourteen, they listen to their parents about 20 percent less every year.

During Zac's campaign, Laurence had noticed he could tell his son to do X or Y, and Zac would ignore him. But if he tapped an expert to deliver the same advice, Zac would apply it.

"It's fascinating, but also frustrating," Laurence said. "You tell your teenagers something and you know that they've heard your words, but you don't know how much actually went in."

And so Bill agreed that while in Cabo, after he'd had a chance to gain Abby's trust, he'd talk to her about the importance of keeping her spirits up. Laurence would later decide that he couldn't have nominated a better person to motivate his daughter.

About ninety miles north of Cabo, Bill spotted the thick cloud layer that formed the leading edge of the forecast storm stalking in off the Pacific. To get below the approaching overcast, Bill descended from ten thousand to about three thousand feet and took the Bonanza east of the Baja peninsula over the Sea of Cortez.

The sun had begun to set, lighting up the cloud bottoms in pink, rose, and gold. Approaching Cabo, the landscape turned more tropical. Off the starboard side of the plane, Laurence could see verdant green mountains plunging toward the sea and whitewater waves crashing against the rocky coast. Bill would have liked to enjoy the view, but instead he radioed Cabo San Lucas tower for landing clearance, lined up on the airport's single runway, and guided the Bonanza to a soft touchdown.

CHAPTER 9
STARTING OVER

CABO SAN LUCAS, BAJA CALIFORNIA, MEXICO
FEBRUARY 2010

 I was really upset about having to stop because of the power issues. On the other hand, I'd been having trouble with my wind gauge, and I could get that fixed too. It would be nice not to have to sail around the world without one. It wasn't like starting, stopping, and starting again hadn't happened to sailors before.

My brother Zac held the record for youngest solo-circumnavigation (with stops) for just six weeks before Michael Perham reset it (he was a few months younger than Zac). Like me, Mike had aimed to sail solo, nonstop, and unassisted. In 2009, he launched from Portsmouth, England, but trouble with his autopilots caused him to have to stop in Lisbon, the Canary Islands, Cape Town, Hobart, and New Zealand. Even with all his stops, Mike still holds the official record for being the youngest man to circumnavigate the world.

The good news about Cabo was that because the city is north of the equator, I could still shoot for the solo, nonstop, unassisted record. After we made the necessary repairs and adjustments, I would simply hit the "reset button" on my attempt, launch from Cabo, circle the world, and land in Cabo at the end. Considering how much time my family and I had spent sailing in Mexico, it seemed kind of appropriate in a way.

On February 3, I approached the southern tip of Baja in the middle of a thick, gray rainstorm. Usually the water in Cabo is a brilliant blue, but that day it was a dull, brownish color. With little wind, I was inching along through curtains of rain that made it really hard to see. With just a few miles to go, the rain let up and I went below to check my gauges. I hadn't been down there long when the blare of a ship's horn nearly blasted me through the cabin roof. Terrified that I'd mistakenly crossed paths with some huge ship, I ran up the companionway, through the cockpit, and onto the rear deck.

Instead of the towering hull of a freighter bearing down on me, I saw a big powerboat at my stern, and my dad standing on the bow laughing and yelling, "G'day, Abigail!"

I was so surprised and happy!

We talked back and forth for a minute, then Dad said, "Hey, start the engine, and let's motor on in."

With the weather like it was, there was no point in trying to sail in, since I was going to be relaunching my solo attempt anyway. So the powerboat, a sixty-four-foot Bertram, took the lead and we motored the rest of the way. As we approached the dock, I got another surprise: a small crowd of people, both Americans and locals, adults and children, waving and yelling out greetings.

"*Viva*, Abby!"

"*Bienvenido!*"

"Hi, Abby! Welcome to Cabo!"

Those people being there gave me such a warm feeling—and maybe took just a tiny bit of the sting out of having to stop.

Steering the boat dockside, I threw a line to Dad, who tied the boat up, then jumped on the boat and gave me a huge hug. Jeff and Scott were standing on the dock, too, along with two other men I'd never met. Dad made the introductions.

"Abby, this is Bill Bennett. He volunteered to fly me down with the batteries. And this is Christopher Golden. It was his boat we brought to meet you."

I thanked Bill and Chris, and that was when the pleasantries stopped and the work began. Jeff and Scott joined us on *Wild Eyes*, and we spent the next couple of hours discussing our plan of attack. It wasn't like they could just load the batteries and fuel aboard and I could sail away again. There was a lot of work to do.

Soon sunset had turned to twilight. The rain started coming down hard again, and we realized we weren't going to get much more done. Plus, everyone was getting pretty hungry. Dad decided to call it a night. One by one, he, Jeff, and Scott stepped off *Wild Eyes*.

But I hung back.

Fiddling with things in the cockpit, finding excuses to delay, I looked reluctantly at the dock. That was when I realized that stepping off the boat a week into my journey had not been in my mental game plan. Without even consciously knowing it, I had wired my brain to stay aboard *Wild Eyes* for six to seven months. Stepping off her now would be like breaking a spell. It felt wrong. I didn't want to do it.

"Abigail."

It was my dad, looking up at me from the dock.

"It's time to go."

Taking a deep breath, I stepped down onto the dock and the spell was broken.

Then came a funny moment: after a week at sea, my land legs were gone. So I didn't *walk* up the dock; I wobbled and tottered and leaned like a drunken . . . um, sailor. If it hadn't been for the guys hoisting me by my foul-weather jacket every so often, I would've fallen flat on my face!

When Abby announced she'd be pulling into Cabo, her critics found a new bone to gnaw on. One blogger wrote:

> Frankly, I don't think her shore team knows [expletive] they are doing. Reading between the lines, she's got all her electronics hot 24/7, including the radar. That's huge energy burn. The chatter is add fuel and batteries, and that's not going to help squat unless she's making stops along the way to refill . . . I am of the opinion that if she loses her electronics, she's dead. She is totally dependent on the shore team for 'what do I do now?' . . . Hmmm . . . we got an electronics expert here (San Diego), a solo sailor here (Bay Area . . .) and someone who built the boat here (Down Under) on this forum. And a bunch of other highly experienced people who have 'been there done that' a number of times. This is the group that knows what they are doing. How do we get the attention of the 'shore team' to make bloody certain this kid doesn't turn into a statistic?[1]

The blogger may have been right that his group knew what they were doing. But his wasn't the only group. Meanwhile, the "chatter" about adding fuel and batteries and the blogger's opinion that "that's not going to help squat unless she's making stops along the way to refill" were dead wrong.

Team Abby's plan was simply meant to increase her storage capacity in order to get her through lulls in sunlight or wind. Rather than relying on statistical weather averages as the previous installer had, they now factored in highs and lows—for example, three to four days of strong, power-generating winds followed by three to four days of light winds. Doubling *Wild Eyes*' storage capacity would ensure Abby could keep her electrical and electronic systems running throughout various weather cycles.

In the end, Team Abby was proven right. Later in Abby's trip, even after *Wild Eyes* lost one wind generator and she was getting no solar power, she was able to keep her systems running by generating electricity in windy conditions, then using battery-stored power in light wind conditions.

While the critical bloggers didn't faze Team Abby, they did begin to bother Ted Caloroso. Ted had come down to Cabo for two reasons. One, to shoot footage for the concept he'd helped sell to Reveille; and two, to finish installing cameras on *Wild Eyes* and train Abby how to use them, a job that was begun, but never finished at Marina del Rey. Even the day before Abby sailed, Jeff Casher still had not seen the cameras—three wired-up camera heads that were to be operated by computer—and the software had not been installed. At 10:00 p.m. the night before Abby sailed, Chris and Ted managed to install two small GoPro cameras on outside mounts. But Abby hadn't been taught how to use the equipment, save any of the images, or transfer them to shore.

Ted did not find the time to finish training Abby on the cameras in Cabo, either. But he did find the time at several points to pull Laurence aside and voice his concerns over whether Abby's boat was properly equipped.

Was *Wild Eyes* fitted with the right power pack? he wanted to know. Why were they adding the marine batteries now? Why were they adding so much fuel? Shouldn't Laurence call in some other experts in the field?

Laurence knew Ted had no sailing experience at all, and suspected he was buying into the opinions of the self-appointed online critics.

"Ted, I'm not calling in any other experts," Laurence finally said. "The experts in the field are here. If they weren't, then we're not who we say we are, and we had no business putting her on the ocean in the first place."

Laurence reminded Ted that he'd just successfully sent his son around the world. "I know what it takes. I know the people I've surrounded myself with. And I know what they're capable of."

For the next three days, Team Abby tackled the *Wild Eyes* workload, laboring from sunup to sundown. Laurence and Bill (who, it turned out, had carpentry expertise) built housings for the new marine batteries, then fiberglassed them in. Repairing the wind sensor turned out to require some extra parts, so Jeff ventured out on a scavenger hunt around Cabo, stopping in at every dinky little shop. His Spanish was really rusty, but even when he could speak the language fairly well, he hadn't learned words like *adaptor* and *amphenol connector*. So that made his shopping trip a bit of a challenge.

The final fix for Abby's wind sensor required someone to go up the mast to replace a corroded connector and recalibrate the sensor with the gauges below. Going up-mast at sea is a dangerous proposition, and many sailors have been killed or badly injured in the process. Even in port going up-mast is best handled as at least a two-person job using a "bosun's chair" and a rope, most often with some form of block-and-tackle pulley system. The chair may be a simple board or some type of rigid sling like a child's swing. While the lucky person picked to go up sits in the seat, another person stands on deck and hoists them, essentially "belaying," the way mountain climbers do, so that a falling climber doesn't fall very far. On *Wild Eyes*, a fall from the top of the mast would be like falling from the fifth floor of an apartment building.

Abby, Laurence, and Christopher Golden (dubbed St. Christopher by then because of his unending aid to Team Abby) each took a turn being hauled up in the bosun's chair to work on the wind sensors. Ironically, Laurence, who is colorblind, went up-mast and connected the colored wires, getting feedback from below when the connections got the sensor running. Then the team hoisted Abby up to help calibrate the sensor. Because she wasn't tall enough to reach the top of the mast, she used a gaff pole to aim the sensor in various directions while the team calibrated it with the gauges below.

The team also repaired Abby's AIS, the transponder system that helped her avoid collisions with other boats. Back at Marina del Rey, installation technicians had gone through three different AIS systems. In Cabo, Jeff began to suspect that the problem might be with a single wire that had been used with all three. He rerouted the wire up through the deck of the boat, glued it to the deck with marine sealant, and ran it down to the equipment without any extra wires. The AIS worked perfectly for the rest of the trip.

While Jeff handled the electronics, Scott was in charge of all things mechanical. But he still had his hand in a cast, so he talked the team through every repair.

 For me, the best part about Cabo was all the new people I met. Like St. Christopher, who from the time I put in, was with us every day, helping us with anything and everything we needed. The port authorities were terrific hosts, even letting Dad and me stay for free in this really nice two-bedroom apartment above the marina offices. Since I was restarting my solo, nonstop attempt in Cabo, I'd be returning there as well. If I made it, it would be a really neat thing for the city.

I also met a sailor named Emily. She was about twenty years old, and ironically, she was from Marina del Rey and had pulled into Cabo to try and piece together an autopilot. She was super laid back, kind of a free spirit who had decided to go on a long sail, but without any particular destination—she was making up her mind as she went. Emily and I had a lot of fun talking. It was great meeting another girl who loved what I love, someone I could relate to.

Another new person I met was Bill Bennett. He was new to the team, but spent the entire three days working like crazy on my boat. I could see that he was really committed to us, not just someone standing up on the dock taking pictures. On my last evening in Cabo, he and I were in *Wild Eyes'* cabin, cleaning up from all the repairs, vacuuming up fiberglass wisps that seemed to have gotten into every nook and cranny.

We had just bagged up the last of them when Bill said, "Hey, walk up to the trash bins with me."

"Okay," I said.

When we reached the top of the dock and tossed the bags into the bins, Bill turned to me with a really serious look on his face. "Abby, your maintaining a positive attitude is going to be more important to the success of your endeavor than navigating the boat, managing the sails, managing the fuel, making water, and keeping the boat sound," he said.

Obviously, I didn't know Bill very well. I wasn't sure he was right that my attitude was *more* important than my boat or my sailing ability. Still, my parents and I had talked a lot about the importance of keeping my spirits up. I wanted to hear Bill's take on the subject.

Bill mentioned Jessica Watson's constant use of the phrase "positive mental attitude," and that got my attention. Jessie and I had talked via e-mail and I respected her as a sailor.

"Every time you feel yourself getting depressed or not feeling good about something, or when something is going to be difficult, you are going to have to turn it around and see the positive side of it," Bill continued. "This is so important that your success depends on it."

"Okay . . ." I said.

"You're going to be in this boat by yourself for six months. You're not going to see another person. It has been proven that prisoners in solitary confinement go crazy."

That got my attention. I looked up at Bill and waited.

"Yes, it's true. So you're going to have to work very hard at keeping yourself positively motivated to do this. Anytime you're starting to feel negative, anytime something bad happens, you personally are going to have to turn it around," Bill said. "There's going to be nobody else there to do that for you."

It was good advice. I would later have many opportunities to use it.

The next morning was my launch day. Just before my launch, the dock gradually started filling up with people again—American ex-pats, American visitors, and Mexican families who had brought their kids to see me off. I was so honored that they came.

After the boat was completely ready, my dad gathered the team below for a moment of prayer. We were a multi-faith group. Dad and me, the evangelical Christians; Scott and Jeff, both Jewish; and Bill, who I later found out was raised in the Catholic Church. We all bowed our heads and my dad prayed that God would keep me safe on my trip. Then each of the guys took turns giving me a hug and saying goodbye.

When it was Bill's turn, I was surprised to see that his eyes were a little red, and it seemed like he was on the verge of tears. Finally he hugged me, and managed to squeeze out just two words: "Come back."

CHAPTER 10
ABBY THE SHELLBACK

CENTRAL AND SOUTH AMERICAN COAST
FEBRUARY–MARCH 2010

 My departure from Cabo happened on a classic Cabo day: blue skies and sunshine, cloudless and clear. St. Christopher invited Team Abby aboard his sixty-four-foot Bertram again so they could escort me out of the harbor. Another big boat, *Cowboy*, also followed us out, along with the harbormaster, who had been so super nice to us.

Because there was very little wind, on my way out of the harbor, I raised full sail. I was just off the westernmost point of the bay, Los Arcos, when the wind filled in—increasing from about five knots to about twenty in a matter of seconds. I went to let my mainsheet out to spill wind and keep the boat from being overpowered, but the mainsheet was jammed in the clutch. *Wild Eyes* rounded up on me causing me to jibe.

A jibe is when your boat turns its stern through the wind so that the wind direction changes from one side of the boat to the other. When that happens, the mainsail and boom swing radically from one side of the boat to the other.

The only thing I could do was to drop the sail, which probably didn't look good to the spectators, but that didn't really matter to me. After regaining control of my boat, I set her back on course and dealt with the jammed clutch on the mainsheet. From then on, a nice fifteen- to twenty-knot wind filled *Wild Eyes'* sails. I looked back at the harbor and was amazed to see the flotilla that had taken the trouble to see me off. I could hear them calling from their boats in English and Spanish.

"*Adios*, Abby!"

"Be safe!"

Over and over, I heard people calling out, "*Vaya con Dios!*" which means, "Go with God!"

Once I got out on the open sea again, several miles from land, the air and sky were *so clean*. On land we think we see things clearly, but there's actually all kinds of stuff in the air that we don't really notice because we're so used to it—dust, mild haze, and sometimes outright smog. At sea there is none of that. Being at sea is like watching the whole world in high-definition. The sky is a deep, forever blue. The clouds, especially the puffy cumulus clouds, are brilliant white, and sail brightly across the sky almost like you're watching a 3-D movie. Those were my conditions for the first few days out of Cabo.

Then it started to rain. Beginning on February 10, squall after squall dumped buckets on me every day. A squall is a small storm—a sudden, sharp increase in wind, often accompanied by rain or thunderstorms. Because I was sailing on a circle of water with horizon in every direction, I could see squalls coming from pretty far off, just black spots out there, looming.

I had choices. I could change course and go around them, but sometimes I'd sail right through them. At night, squalls were a real pain because it could be dead calm out and I'd be below sleeping, then all of a sudden I would hear the wind building. Within five minutes the wind would spike to thirty or even forty knots. I had to sprint topside, drop a ton of sail and run through all the dozens of little changes required to sail in those conditions. Then ten minutes later, the storm would be gone.

On February 10, Commanders' notified us of a low-pressure system developing to the southwest. Low-pressure systems cough up all kinds of bad weather: higher winds, steady rain showers, thunderstorms. I was trying to avoid this one by passing the area to the west. Commanders' was routing another boat in my vicinity, about three hundred miles southwest of me. I found out it was getting smashed with fifty-to seventy-knot winds. This boat had a family aboard traveling to the South Pacific. They had gone "hove to," and were riding it out.

"Heaving to" is when you turn the boat into the wind and set the helm and sails in such a way that you don't need to steer. Then, ideally, you can go below and ride out the storm. It's a balancing act because you have to set up the boat so that you're not making forward progress, but you're not going backward either. As I said, I occasionally tried to steer around the squalls. I have to admit, though, when I heard there might be some unavoidable nasty weather ahead, I was kind of excited.

I had been waiting around for a good storm. I'd been in some bad weather, I knew the boat backward and forward, and I thought, *Maybe this is gonna be it! My first real storm!*

That might sound crazy, but I guess it's like any other sport. The minor league baseball player who wants to make it to the big leagues. The small-time race car driver who thinks he's ready for NASCAR. I wanted to test myself. It was exciting to be heading into something new. That's what my whole trip was about: getting out here and experiencing stuff that I couldn't experience while sailing back and forth between Catalina and Marina del Rey.

On February 12, four days out of Cabo, I encountered the strongest winds I'd had so far, about thirty-five knots. Also, I saw another side of the normally tranquil Pacific Ocean. Massive walls of water began rising up behind me, each one looking like a giant blue slide at a water park. Each swell looked like it was going to crash over my whole boat. But because of the way *Wild Eyes* was built, the swells propelled us forward in a surge of speed and we surfed down the wave fronts. These were *real* water slides twenty-five feet high, and sometimes I'd be zinging down them going at least twenty knots. It was way more addicting than surfing at the beach!

The downside to the low-pressure system was that it was like being closed up in a giant bowl where everything you see is gray. The line between the water and the clouds blurred together, erasing the horizon. Some days a dense, soupy fog dropped over the boat, so thick that I could stand in the cockpit and just barely see the bow. On a few days I couldn't even see past the dodger. It was like sailing inside a grey envelope. I made sure my chart plotter and AIS were on, but I was still thinking, *Man, I hope there's no uncharted land out there!*

I mean, I knew intellectually that there was nothing around me for hundreds of miles. But it's still reassuring to be able to actually *see* for miles around with the eyes God gave you, instead of relying on machines.

I had a Thrane & Thrane Sailor 250 FleetBroadband satellite communication system onboard, one of my lines to the outside world. There was a big dome on the back of my boat with a little antenna inside; and down below there was a little phone and cable that I could hook up to my computer and get online. My mom sent me out blog comments occasionally from people who were following my trip, and I loved reading them. It made me feel really cared for.

There was this one person whose blogger name was "Jony the Pony."

He (or she?) called me "Babsy," which other bloggers picked up on, and kept me entertained with random, off-the-wall comments. There were a lot of young kids who were inspired that I was trying to sail around the world alone. Plus, there were a lot of older people who would say things like, "I'm glad you're getting to do this. I wish I had been able to when I was younger." So it was cool because through the comments, I could see that my trip was inspiring all different kinds of people, maybe even giving them ideas for their own exciting adventures.

Lots of little kids would send me questions too. Typical kid questions like, "What do you do when you're bored?" "Where do you go to the bathroom?" "Is the 'mast' that pointy thing that sticks up in the air?"

Then I found out something that amazed me: a group of NASA scientists was following my trip. Here I was, just this kid out here having fun on a sailboat, and there were all these super-brainy people who had designed the satellite-linked equipment I was using and they wanted to see how well it works. I thought it was pretty neat that my little adventure would interest them.

Using the Thrane & Thrane was crazy expensive, but I had a little bit of sponsored time. I forget how much, exactly, but enough to check e-mail and occasionally go on Facebook, and maybe look at some pictures of me hanging out with my friends. I usually saved the time for when I was having a really bad day, but most of the time I liked being alone. I've always liked sailing alone, the responsibility of running my own ship, and in that way, sort of running my own life.

Now that I'm thinking about it, maybe that was why I was attracted to soloing. During "normal" life ashore, being around people made me nervous, and I didn't talk a lot. Even when I grew into my teens, I wasn't very confident. I was afraid of messing up and embarrassing myself. I didn't like being in a position where I had to make decisions in front of other people. So when other people were around, I would kind of sit back and let them decide.

The ocean was different. The ocean was my comfort zone, and whenever I was out on the water, I was really confident, especially when I was alone. I think that's because everything was my responsibility, and I knew it, so when problems came up, I didn't hesitate to tackle them and try new solutions. And a good percentage of the time, I'd get it right.

Like my alternator belt, for example. My engine was working great, but the one thing about it that drove me crazy was this alternator belt that had to be tightened about once a week. To do the job, I had to cram myself into a space that was like one-foot square, and hang over the engine with wrenches and all sorts of stuff, then loosen this one bolt while holding the alternator out to tighten the belt, then tighten the bolt while holding the belt. Meanwhile, the boat would be rolling all over the place. And I needed one hand to hold the belt and two hands to tighten the bolt, which meant I was one hand short for the job. But after a while, I got pretty good at it. I could do it pretty fast and get it right the first time.

It was those kinds of experiences, those little victories, that built my confidence in myself.

I heard a story once where a young guy says to an older man, "Hey, how did you get so successful?"

"By making good decisions," the older man answers.

"How did you learn to make good decisions?"

"From experience," the older man says.

"Well, how did you get the experience?"

The older man looks at the young man and says, "By making bad decisions."

It seems like people my age are over-protected today. Even to the point where a lot of parents refuse to put their kids in the position to make important decisions, to aspire to great things, because they don't want to put them in a position to fail. I mean, there are all these mini-vans driving down the road with bumper stickers that say, "My child was

Student of the Week at Smith Elementary," or whatever. But guess what? *Every* child gets to be student of the week. It's like we, as kids, aren't expected or required to reach higher, to be different, to do anything special in order to get some kind of warm, fuzzy award. It's just weird.

When this country was founded, guys my age were running farms or apprenticing in a trade or going to war. Girls my age were starting families. Now we're supposed to have "teenage years," which seems to mean you go to high school, maybe play a sport or learn an instrument. If you belong to a church, you might go on mission trips to foreign countries, which is cool. Other than that, it's hang out at the mall, surf the Internet, and wait until you're eighteen to start your life.

As I passed weeks alone at sea, especially when watching amazing sunsets or night skies filled with shooting stars, I was so thankful that my parents trusted me enough, and had enough faith in my abilities, to let me follow my passion and try to do something great, even if I might fail. And it was little successes along the way that changed me, built my confidence, and helped me grow.

 The Sunderlands aren't sure when Ted Caloroso jumped ship. But sometime between Cabo and mid-February, he contacted Reveille, the production company that had bought the rights to Magnetic's reality-show concept, and convinced its executives to abandon the project.

In what appeared to be a press release published on a sailing website, Ted would later claim that "Abby's journey ran into trouble in Cabo San Lucas in March 2010." (This although Abby departed Cabo on February 7.) The release went on to state that Ted, who as far as the Sunderlands knew, had no sailing experience, "witnessed what he believed to be a lack of preparation, lack of training, and an overall disregard for the safety of Abby by the Sunderland family. Accordingly, both Magnetic and its corporate partner in the endeavor, Reveille, determined it was necessary to terminate the project at that time in an effort to discourage the Sunderland family from continuing to put Abby at risk. Nevertheless, Abby's journey continued."[1]

Despite the claims made in the release, Ted Caloroso's interest in producing a show on Abby's journey also continued. On March 8, 2010, Ted, along with Magnetic's Chris Bates, signed a "reversion" agreement with Reveille, meaning that Reveille was relinquishing its rights to the Sunderlands' story.

A few days later, Laurence Sunderland got a phone call. It was Ted Caloroso. He'd formed a new company, 23 South Productions, he said, and wanted the rights to the Sunderlands' story.

Strange, Laurence thought. *Why would Ted go behind Chris's back and ask us to sign with him? I thought they were friends.*

Laurence and Marianne discussed this odd development. They decided to call Chris and ask him what was up. On a Friday evening in late March, the Sunderlands met with Chris Bates.

"I don't know how to tell you this," Chris said, "but Ted is convinced that Abigail will die out there, and he wants to do an exposé on your family."

Laurence and Marianne were stunned.

"He's going to throw you under the bus," Chris continued. "He wants to put you in jail for being reckless and endangering your daughter, and he thinks he's going to make millions."

After that, Ted Caloroso kept calling the Sunderlands, leaving messages that said he still wanted the rights to Abby's story. The Sunderlands did not return his calls.

 For a lot of sailors, the hardest part of a voyage is the Doldrums. The Doldrums run along the equator in an area meteorologists call the Intertropical Convergence Zone.

That's a fancy way of saying that tropical winds from the northern and southern hemispheres go head to head in a weather war and neither side wins. When you're in a sailboat, especially on a nonstop attempt, your whole purpose in life is to find wind and make way. But in the Doldrums, the sea is dead calm and silent, and the windless days can go on for weeks.

As I sailed farther south, nearer and nearer the equator, the days turned steamy and miserable. I lived in swimsuits and poured buckets of saltwater over my head to try to cool off. But the water itself was like eighty degrees, so that didn't help much.

I was sweating even when it was pouring rain. On the upside, the rain was so warm I could shower in it! Because there was so much moisture in the air, the raindrops were huge; and because the sea was so flat, the drops hit the water with these fat, plopping sounds. If it rained really hard, the sky turned a deep charcoal gray and the giant drops chewed the surface of the sea into an ugly gray mess.

Soon I was so far south that it was too hot to stay inside the cabin. So I stuffed a beanbag chair inside a sail bag, put it in the cockpit, and sat out there watching blue-footed boobies dive for fish. They were so cute, with white breasts, dark gray wings, and sky-blue legs and feet. They were good company. At night I even slept out there in the cockpit, waves splashing over me, occasionally getting hit by a fish that surfed in. As hot and miserable as I was, getting smacked by a fish was only a minor annoyance. After all, he was just passing through.

At that point, I was really looking forward to getting farther south into cooler weather. But I knew I'd probably wish the opposite when I was in the Southern Ocean, freezing my tail off.

When it wasn't raining, the humidity did incredible things to the sun. At sunset, if there were clouds on the horizon, they seemed to pull at the sun's edges, stretching it wider and brushing its top into a blurry fringe. The sun looked like it was melting down into the clouds in a warm, reddish gold that reached across the water all the way to my boat. Then, slowly, the sun slipped below the horizon, pulling the light across the water with it, until it was just a fiery red line between the sea and the twilight.

On February 19, all the sluggish winds and steamy heat I'd endured became worth it: I officially went from being Abby the Pollywog to Abby the Shellback. That's been a big moment in sailors' lives for centuries, and it happens when you cross the equator. Before you cross, you're just a Slimy Pollywog. After you cross, you become a Trusty Shellback. In the American and British navies, they still make a huge deal out of it with a two-day "Crossing the Line" ceremony, where the sailors who are already Shellbacks torture the Wogs with fraternity-type pranks.

Since I was a single-hander, I had my own little ceremony and video-taped it. At the moment I "crossed the line," I poured a bucket of warm saltwater over my head. Of course, I had been doing that for the last hundred miles, but to me, this was *special* saltwater—it came right off the equator!

I was happy to be a Shellback because crossing the line was really the first big landmark of my trip. Except for my little ceremony, though, that day was not fun. The winds were nearly zero and when I did cross the line, I was traveling at about the speed of a land turtle. Worse, once I was just south of the equator, the wind died completely, and a current caught *Wild Eyes*. Suddenly, I was drifting north again. I'd already crossed the equator once that day—I did not want a do-over!

Going below, I looked at my chart plotter and could see where the line was. Then I hopped back up on deck and eyeballed that approximate spot in the ocean, mentally turning the water north of the line a different color of blue. For a good half-hour I stood there staring off the back of the boat, caught helpless in the northbound current.

I can't see the equator, I thought. *But I know it's there and I better not go back over it!*

I estimate I had gotten within about a football field's length of it when, as if God heard my desperation, the wind picked up. *Wild*

Eyes started moving south again, and I was officially in the Southern Hemisphere. My next goal: Cape Horn, the southernmost tip of South America, 4,800 miles away.

On February 27, I was more than a thousand miles off the coast of Chile, when my phone rang. It was my mom. She said a massive earthquake had just rocked Chile, killing hundreds and generating tsunami warnings in fifty-three countries. The U.S. Coast Guard had called to check on me because they'd received a lot of phone calls from people who were following my trip. Mom said a lot of people had posted worried comments on my blog asking if I might be in the path of a killer wave.

At the time, I was in about three thousand feet of water, so I knew that even if a tsunami was building in my neighborhood, it would pass underneath me and I probably wouldn't feel anything. Just to be safe, I gave *Wild Eyes* a very thorough once-over, checking my sails, pins, and lines, and making sure all my hatches were sealed up tight. But none of that kept me from picturing what a tsunami might look like if it did rise up and roar toward my little boat like some watery blue version of the Great Wall of China.

CHAPTER 11

AROUND THE HORN

THE SOUTHERN OCEAN
MARCH 2010

 As I sailed parallel to the South American coast, it was important to stay far enough offshore to avoid the accelerated winds near the coast of Chile. I hit several milestones. On March 14th, I sailed across the 40th line of latitude, putting me into the "Roaring 40s." The sky was suppose to turn black, the winds roaring, waves crashing around me! But none of that happened . . . the weather was calm and boring. Next thing I knew I'd be rounding Cape Horn, the dreaded Mt. Everest of sailing, lounging on deck in a swimsuit, reading a book!

On March 17, St. Patrick's Day, the 40s started to behave themselves and gave me a nice windy gale. Just a small one, but I took advantage of it and ran topside in my red foul-weather gear to snap some pictures. The wind kept blowing my hood off my head, letting every wave that hit go right down my jacket. In minutes, my fingers were so numb I couldn't push the buttons on my camera!

A week later, still paralleling South America about a thousand miles offshore, I crossed the 50th line of latitude into the infamous "Furious 50s." Um . . . not all that furious.

For the first couple of days, I rolled around in sloppy seas with barely any wind at all. On the other hand, the temperatures dove into the fifties. I went from wishing for ice at the equator to watching out for ice in the waters around me.

South and west of Chile, and now out of the Pacific and in the Southern Ocean for real, it was like I had been watching a play and someone suddenly changed the set. Around me the whole world was dark and gray, the horizon lines blending into the sky. And omigosh, was it cold. Cold and wet and really windy. There were a few quiet days, but the thing I remember most about being down there was the whip-like wind flinging ocean spray everywhere. Sometimes I couldn't tell if it was raining or just spray off the sea because the water splattered in from all different directions.

And did I mention it was cold?

There wasn't really any way to get to the point of being what a normal person would call "warm," because everything, including my clothes, was always soaking wet. That's something you don't think much about while living at home in a regular neighborhood: just the blessing of being dry.

At sea, I had no real way to dry my clothes. I mean, occasionally I would run my heater and hang some clothes in front of it. But the heater sucked up fuel and I didn't want to use it all. Also, if I ran the heater, I'd be wearing fewer layers while below in the cabin. That meant if something happened outside—like a jibe from my autopilots—and I needed to jump out there and deal with it, I'd be freezing cold and soaked through, with another batch of wet clothes and no way to dry them. After a few experiences like that, I decided to outfit myself for all weather and all situations. Even while below, I wore my foul-weather gear over all my layers and just left the portlight, a small cabin window, open. Without the heater, it was as cold below as it was outside, anyway. At least this way, if I needed to run topside, I'd be ready to go.

For example, on March 26, a few days out of Cape Horn, my main autopilot malfunctioned. I tried switching to the backup, but it didn't help. It was way past midnight back home and I didn't want to wake up the team. So I decided to hand steer for a few hours. During a break, I went below and e-mailed Scott:

TO: "ABBY'S INTERNAL LIST"
SUBJECT: AUTOPILOT ISSUE

HEY SCOTT,
    I'M HAVING A LITTLE TROUBLE WITH MY AUTOPILOT. THERE IS A LOT OF PINK TRANSMISSION FLUID BACK THERE ON THE HULL, I'M NOT SURE WHAT THE PROBLEM IS, EXACTLY. I HOOKED UP THE BACK-UP AUTOPILOT BUT THAT WON'T EVEN TURN ON. IT LIGHTS UP BUT THE SCREEN STAYS BLANK WHICH DOESN'T MAKE SENSE, SINCE I WAS USING IT JUST A FEW WEEKS AGO . . . I'VE BEEN HAND STEERING SINCE ABOUT 10 PACIFIC TIME, BUT IT'S STARTING TO GET A LITTLE COLD OUT THERE AND I KNOW YOU HARDLY EVER SLEEP SO I THOUGHT I'D SHOOT YOU A QUICK E-MAIL AND SEE IF YOU'RE STILL UP. IF I HAVEN'T FROZEN TO DEATH BY TOMORROW, WE SHOULD DEFINITELY TALK ABOUT THE WIND GENERATOR ON THE PHONE. I'M STARTING TO GET A LITTLE CONFUSED MYSELF . . .

I hit "send," then climbed back up into the cockpit. Scrunching down low, I tried to stay safe at the tiller while watching the compass and wind gauge to keep myself on course. The sky and sea were pitch black. That night, the concept of "cold" took on an entirely new meaning for me. I had maybe thirty-five or forty knots of freezing wind with icy waves crashing over the boat, one after the other. I was wearing a bunch of layers—high-tech thermal pants and shirts and stuff, with my foul-weather gear over all that. But the waves kept dumping right on top of me, pouring down my neck and splashing up my pants. The water was so cold it felt like it had come straight from a glacier, and I was so wet that I might as well have been swimming.

Also, my hands were completely numb. Even though I had gloves on, water managed to get inside them, and I couldn't feel my fingers. This wasn't necessarily a bad thing: my hands were covered with tiny cuts from all the maintenance work I'd been doing, and because I was always wet, they'd become infected. At least with my hands numb, I couldn't feel the pain.

Wild Eyes was rocking all over the place in the pitch black. I could sometimes catch a wave and surf its front. But then another wave would hit me on the beam and knock me sideways. It was like sailing inside a giant washing machine. That part was kind of fun. I was miserably cold, but I wasn't scared. Losing your technology isn't the end of the world. *Wild Eyes* was handling fine, so I hand steered for a few more hours then called the team. It turned out that there was an electrical problem with the autopilot. Jeff talked me through a quick repair and I was on my way.

I felt good about toughing it out that night, then following it up with a successful repair. It really built my confidence.

During that same run down the coast of South America, I had my first accidental jibe as a single-hander on the open sea. It's the worst feeling in the world when you feel the stern swing around, knowing that an uncontrolled boom slamming to the other side of the boat will hit the running backstays that are partially responsible for holding up the mast. If the boom hits hard enough it could take out the backstays, damage or break the boom, or even bring down the mast.

In this case, it was the middle of the night and I was sailing along in a squall, just a heavy shower. I had gone below to check my chart plotter and radar when I felt the boat beginning to get overpowered by the wind. Then she started to swing around.

I jumped up and ran topside into a rain shower with fat drops the size of jelly beans. In seconds I was soaking wet. Since the wind was gusting, I began "sheeting out." That's when you make the sail looser so that it "spills" wind instead of catching it, because if the sail is too taut, a sharp gust can knock your boat over. I sat in the cockpit with curtains of rain crossing my deck in fat splatters, and sheeted out as much as I could then started to reef. My mainsail had three "reefing points" in it. "Reefing down" is how you make the mainsail smaller.

I had two reefs in the main and headed below to get out of the rain. While adjusting my course by the autopilot controls, a sudden gust hit and the autopilot snapped into standby mode. I saw the loose tiller jolt hard to the side as the boat began to spin. I jumped outside to grab the tiller but it was too late. *Wild Eyes* jibed to starboard. The boom swung from left to right and hit the running backstay. Heart pounding, I grabbed the tiller and quickly got us back on course.

After that, I hand steered for a while until the squall passed, then I put out some more sail. Commanders' Weather had forecast no more squalls for the night, but I went below and flipped on my radar just in case. It was my first serious jibe and it was a little scary. Looking back now, I had no idea that night what scary really meant.

 The distance between Thousand Oaks, California, and Ushuaia, Tierra del Fuego, Argentina, is 6,846 miles. But that calculation is "as the crow flies," and Laurence Sunderland would not be making the trip on a crow. Instead, on March 24, he drove an hour from Thousand Oaks to Marina del Rey, then took a taxi to

LAX (which is not as easy as it sounds, depending on the snarl of Los Angeles traffic). After inching through security queues and a two-hour wait in the terminal, he boarded an airline called Lan Chile and flew eleven hours to Santiago, Chile, then took a connecting flight to the international airport in Buenos Aires, Argentina. Air-wise from Buenos Aires to Ushuaia, the saying held true: you can't get there from here . . . unless you take a hair-raising ride with an Argentine taxi driver. Laurence did, hanging on tight through the labyrinthine streets of Buenos Aires to another little airport from which small planes would ferry paying passengers to Tierra del Fuego, which is often called the "End of the Earth."

Laurence had already sailed and traveled to so many places in the world that he didn't need to see another magnificent snowy peak or ride a boat down some new and exotic waterway. He didn't even particularly care about seeing Cape Horn. All he wanted was to be there when his daughter conquered the Cape. He wanted to say "Hello! Great job!" He wanted to give her a boost.

He also hoped to film Abby's record-breaking passage and had brought along a couple of fancy cameras to do the job. Reveille had reversed its rights to Magnetic Entertainment's proposed television program, and the Sunderlands had declined to work further with Ted Caloroso. After the reversion, Chris Bates presented the Sunderlands with a new contract that would have given him the rights to continue shopping a reality show. Though Laurence and Marianne liked and trusted Chris, they had decided to steer clear of Hollywood for the time being. But they still wanted a video record of Abby's trip.

Being the youngest person to solo around Cape Horn would be a major accomplishment, and the Sunderlands wanted to document it. Aboard *Wild Eyes*, Abby had some GoPro "point of view" cameras and two Canon High Definition video cameras. Together with footage shot in Marina del Rey and Cabo, along with Abby's homecoming, film of her rounding the Horn would make a treasured keepsake.

The Sunderlands' Argentina contact, John Selby, picked up Laurence from the airport and took him to his home for a meal. After that, it was off to an inexpensive hotel for the night. Laurence remembers being so exhausted by then that he felt as if his eyeballs were literally hanging out of his head.

The next morning, John introduced Laurence to Ian Upsall, an Aussie skipper who had agreed to motor south from Cape Horn to try to connect father and daughter on this historic segment of her journey. Laurence, Ian, and two other crew members got underway on Ian's boat, *Persimmon*, sailing east along the Beagle Channel.

Running east and west near the extreme southern point of South America, the Beagle Channel is 130 miles long, but at its narrowest point is just over three miles wide. The strait connects the Pacific and Atlantic oceans, and its eastern portion forms part of the border between Chile and Argentina. Named for the HMS *Beagle*, the ship on which Charles Darwin made his famous passage to the Galapagos Islands, the channel and its scenery change like a kaleidoscope. In some spots jagged, glacier-laced mountains plunge into steely seas. Elsewhere glaciers have carved out narrow fjords now flanked by hills of bright green. And in other places along the channel, tiny islands rise from water dyed a deep cobalt blue.

Headed east toward the Atlantic, Ian piloted *Persimmon* about seventy-five miles down the channel. As evening fell, he put in at a tiny cove where green hills rose from rocky shores. The air was fresh and cold and perfectly still. On the beach lay piles of driftwood so ancient and bleached that they looked to Laurence as if they had been there since Darwin sailed by.

 I knew my dad had traveled all the way to Ushuaia, the capital of Tierra del Feugo Province, Argentina. Ushuaia is usually considered the southernmost populated city in the world. Traveling on his British passport, Dad had taken who knew how many taxis, planes, and boats to get there, just so he could motor out a hundred miles into the South Atlantic and watch me achieve a big part of my dream.

To keep my voyage in the record-setting category of "unassisted," Dad would not be able to set foot on *Wild Eyes* or give me any kind of supplies or even a hug. All he would be able to do was watch, wave, take pictures, and yell, "G'day, Abigail!" It meant so much to me that he would travel all that way just to see me for what would probably amount to a few minutes' time—but probably what would be some of the most important minutes I would ever experience.

On the night of March 30, I was only one day out of Cape Horn. I was beginning to get excited about completing the second significant leg of my trip. First, the equator; now about to become the youngest person ever to round the Horn solo and unassisted. I set my sails and the autopilot on the course that would take me to meet my dad the next day. Just as I was thinking about getting some sleep, the autopilot malfunctioned, causing *Wild Eyes* to jibe.

Then the autopilot started shifting headings radically, steering me first in one direction, then another.

I jumped up top, got back on course, let down some sail, then tried to reset the autopilot via the remote mounted in the cockpit. But it was like the machine had lost its mind or something. Suddenly *Wild Eyes* was all over the place. I grabbed the tiller, steered us on course, and jumped below to the main autopilot. Just as I reached it, the screen went dead.

Time to switch to the backup, I thought.

Speed-crawling to the stern, I plugged in the drive that connects the secondary autopilot to the tiller, turned it on, and got that set up. Then I crawled back to the forward pilot compartment and switched on the "brain" for the secondary.

Nothing happened.

It wasn't steering the boat. To check this, I went topside. When the autopilot is working, the ram—a rod that attaches the autopilot to the rudder—moves the tiller and holds it on course. I grabbed the tiller and sure enough, I could move it any which way I wanted.

Great, I thought. *I'm one-hundred-fifty miles off Cape Horn, both autopilots are broken, and my boat is drifting toward one of the nastiest chunks of ocean on the face of the earth.*

I could've heaved to and stopped for the night, but I was supposed to meet my dad the next day. It was only about 5:00 p.m. back in Thousand Oaks, so I decided to call the team.

 At 5:00 p.m. on Tuesday, March 30, Scott Lurie was just pulling his truck into his driveway when Marianne's number popped up on his cell phone.

"Hello?"

"Hi, Scott. Abby just called and said she's having serious autopilot problems. She said you should call her, and if not, she'll call you."

Scott immediately hung up and dialed Abby's sat phone. Abby got right to it: "I have no power at all to pilot A, and pilot B either has no power or isn't working right because I can still hand steer the boat even with the autopilot engaged."

For the next hour, Scott did not leave his truck, but sat in his driveway troubleshooting a problem seven thousand miles away, basically in the blind. The first thing he asked Abby to do was check to see if the "brain box" of the main autopilot had power.

"Go get your volt meter," he said.

Silence on the line for a few moments, then Abby said, "I got it out of my tool bag, but it won't turn on."

"The batteries are probably dead," Scott said. "Do you have a spare 9-volt battery?"

A few more moments of scratchy silence, then Abby was back with bad news: "I took off the back. The whole thing's full of water."

Not a surprise, especially in a boat like Abby's, where the cabin floor was the actual bilge—or the lowest part of the boat where its two sides meet—and had at least a half-inch of water sloshing around at almost all times. And when the boat was heeled way over, much of the bulkhead, or wall, was below the waterline. There was almost nothing aboard a boat like hers that might not wind up wet.

Still, it was a big blow to the troubleshooting process.

Great, Scott thought. *We've got to electrically troubleshoot an autopilot and we don't even have a volt meter.*

Troubleshooting equipment is like following a breadcrumb trail. First Scott had Abby cycle through a few switches to see whether the display would come alive on pilot A or B. When she pushed X button, does Y light come on? That kind of thing, just following the system's circuit to learn where the electrical power was hitting a wall.

About a half-hour into the call, Scott got Jeff on the line to help. The electronics, or "brains," of *Wild Eyes'* autopilots were located in a couple of far aft compartments. There were two systems, A and B, a primary and a backup. Each contained a motherboard, exactly like a computer, plus a CPU and numerous connectors. Each system also had an LED display with a control panel. The system's brains were electrically wired to a pair of mechanical motors, or "drives," in a cramped compartment at the very back of the boat. Each drive was equipped with a rod that moved in and out hydraulically and steered the rudder. In addition to the brains, displays, and drives, the system included a compass and a remote control. The remote control was located topside in the cockpit.

There is a long list of expertise a sailor has to have in order to single-hand around the world. Repairing a complex electrical/electronic/hydraulic system isn't one of them. It would turn out that Abby would have to do much more than that.

Persimmon emerged from the eastern mouth of the Beagle Channel into the South Atlantic. Laurence had been checking in frequently with Marianne to get an update on Abby's position so that he and Ian could plot a course to intercept her. On the third day out, Marianne told Laurence that *Wild Eyes'* autopilots had gone haywire and that Jeff and Scott were troubleshooting the problem with Abby by telephone.

Laurence did not call in with any advice. Not only did he have complete confidence in the two men, but as a veteran shipwright he had learned that adding more ingredients to an already difficult recipe usually didn't help. Too many cooks, etcetera.

Still, the news immediately spurred Laurence to prayer. No single-hander wants to be without an autopilot. And no sailor at all wants to be without an autopilot while navigating the treacherous waters around Cape Horn.

An Englishman himself, Laurence had learned as a schoolboy about Sir Francis Drake, one of the world's first circumnavigators. Queen Elizabeth I commissioned Drake (a hero to the English; to the Spanish, a notorious pirate) to lead the first English sail around the world. By the time he reached the southernmost tip of South America in 1577, Drake's convoy of six ships had already been cut to three. Violent storms through the Straits of Magellan destroyed a fourth ship and forced another to return to England, leaving only Drake's flagship to continue west into the Pacific, through the area now called Drake's passage.

The passage around Cape Horn has terrorized sailors through all centuries since. That's because storms that form in the Indian Ocean build energy as they pass eastbound under Australia, scream into the Southern Ocean unchecked by any landmass, then finally unleash their full fury beneath South America. In ancient shanties, seamen sang about sailing the turbulent waters there, often rhyming "Cape Horn" with verses in which they wished they'd "never been born."

Today, the Chilean navy maintains a station on *Isla Hoorn*. Not far from it stands a sobering reminder of the Cape's dangerous waters: a sculpture of an albatross, a memorial to the many sailors who have perished there.

 I spent the whole night on the phone with Jeff and Scott, switching wires and components back and forth, testing each new configuration again and again. They would tell me what to do and I would do it. I was moving these tiny colored wires around between tiny connectors. Often, just as I would line up a wire and a hole, the boat would pitch wildly and I'd miss and have to start all over.

The aft compartment that houses all of the autopilot components was actually divided into two small spaces. Both were tiny, and I had to lie on my back in an inch of freezing water, holding my flashlight in my teeth, pointing it up at the brain box, and making adjustments with a little jeweler's screwdriver. I had to go back and forth between compartments—aft to the autopilot drive and forward to the "brains" again. At one point while working on the drive, I tucked the jeweler's screwdriver in a little niche and made a mental note of it. But then *Wild Eyes* pitched crazily and when I got back to the aft compartment, the screwdriver was gone.

The rest of the screwdrivers in my tool bag were too big for this detailed work, so I dug around until I found my nail clippers, the kind with one of those little files that flips out. It would have to do.

Whenever frustration started sniffing around inside me, I shut it off like a light switch.

I am where I am and this is what it is, I told myself. *You can either suck it up and work the problem or hand steer to the nearest land.*

For me, the second option was no option at all.

TOP RIGHT: Catalina Island. I was about
sixteen months old here and had lived
onboard since I was five months old.

ABOVE: On the bow of *Amazing Grace*,
my favorite place while at sea. I was
about nine years old.

RIGHT: Onboard *Amazing Grace* during
our trip down in Mexico. *Left to Right:*
Zac, dinner (a big, fat Dorado), my dad,
and me.

Crewing on a Catalina 30 when I was thirteen years old.

Riding with my little brother Ben on my horse Czar when I was fifteen.

ABOVE: In Rhode Island, right before leaving Newport on our way down the coast to Florida. *Left to Right:* Trond Hjerto, my Dad, Zac, and me.

RIGHT: An exciting time waiting and watching from the Mexican panga as *Wild Eyes* was lifted off of the *Marie Rickmers* in Ensenada, Mexico!

Work started as soon as *Wild Eyes* arrived in Marina del Rey.

ABOVE: The entire team worked night and day right up until the day I left.

RIGHT: We decided to paint a red heart on the bottom of *Wild Eyes* to make her more visible from the air in the event of a capsize.

Working on the rigging during one of my sea trials. This was one of my favorite places on *Wild Eyes*.

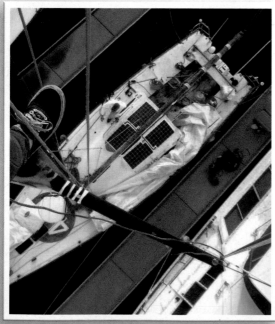

View from the top of the mast.

Courtesy of the Sunderland family

Off on my first solo sea trial.

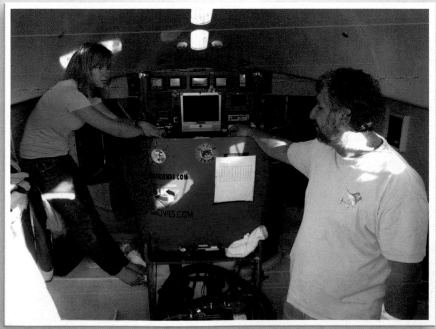

Bill Bennett, ASC

Down below talking with Team Abby member Scott Lurie. (Navigation station to my left and the engine to my right.)

Departure day and the press conference at the Del Rey Yacht Club. *Left to right:* Zac, me, Mom, and Dad.

Sailing out of Marina del Rey on January 23rd—finally!

Dad and Team members Scott Lurie and Bill Bennett taking a break from repairs in Cabo San Lucas, Mexico. *Left to Right:* Laurence Sunderland, Scott Lurie, and Bill Bennett.

Talking over the list of work after pulling into Cabo.

Wild Eyes under full sail in light wind.

Bill Bennett, ASC

Restarting my solo nonstop attempt from Cabo San Lucas, Mexico, with Los Arcos to starboard.

Abby Sunderland

Abby Sunderland

Abby Sunderland

UPPER LEFT: Sitting on my boom enjoying a beautiful day.

UPPER RIGHT: In the cockpit at dusk just after crossing the equator.

BOTTOM: Sailing in the southern ocean!

Eben Human

Real food for the first time in three months thanks to the fabulous Cape Grace Hotel, South Africa.

Laurence Sunderland

Leaving Cape Town, South Africa, after nearly two weeks of repairs with the landmark Table Mountain to port.

Will Blackshaw and Michael Wear aboard the Qantas A330 Search and Rescue flight after locating and communicating with me.

From the French fishing vessel *Ile de la Reunion* as it arrives on the scene with me standing in the cockpit of the dismasted *Wild Eyes*.

This close-up photo of me in the cockpit of *Wild Eyes* shows the extent of the damage from being rolled 360 degrees.

Captain LeMoigne and crew from the *Ile de la Reunion* approach *Wild Eyes*.

Stepping off the French patrol vessel *Osiris,* with my brother Zac after an eleven-day bash through the Indian Ocean to Reunion Island.

Jeff, Zac, and I after messing around on jet skis on Reunion Island.

Press conference back in Marina del Rey, the morning after I got home.

The whole family together again the night I got home.

My baby brother Paul-Louis arrived just twelve hours after I got home! My parents named him after Captain Paul-Louis LeMoigne of the *Ile de la Reunion*.

Jeff and Scott were amazed at Abby's coolness under pressure. Despite being thrown around the cabin by some of the roughest seas on earth, and trying new, different—and sometimes the same—solutions over and over and over again, never once did her voice waiver.

Never once did she complain, lose her temper, or grumble something like, "But we already tried that!"

Neither man ever sensed the slightest hint of frustration. Abby sounded as if this was just another thing to get through.

Because of his circumnavigation experience, Jeff knew that *Wild Eyes* would be drifting and spinning with the currents, changing angles, getting dowsed with wave after wave from the stern, bow, and beam. He knew Abby would be sitting or lying on the floor in a half-inch or more of water, one minute rocking side to side, the next pitching along in the direction of the waves. He also knew that condensation would cause *Wild Eyes'* gear to drip, drip, drip on her constantly.

"I had to always remind myself that she is getting thrown around the whole time we were talking to her," Jeff would later say. "And you would never know that from her voice."

Seventy-five percent of the veteran male sailors Jeff knew wouldn't have even made it through the diagnosis, much less the ten-hour marathon that none of them could have foreseen.

As the troubleshooting entered its fifth hour, Abby had drifted closer to the tight cluster of islands that forms the southern tip of Chile. Jeff and Scott became concerned about some of them, which were really more like giant rocks. The closest was just twenty miles away.

Over the years, Jeff had done a number of marine rescues via radio. He knew that he and Scott had a responsibility to sound calm, to never let Abby think they were nervous or worried.

"Abby, take a look at your chart plotter and check your position," Jeff said mildly.

She responded—latitude, longitude, degrees.

Back in California, Jeff plotted her position and monitored it carefully. The winds were blowing from west to east, pushing Abby's boat
toward the rocks as she struggled with the autopilots below. If *Wild
Eyes* reached those islands, she wouldn't run aground, keel in the sand.
She would be smashed into pieces.

 I could hear the wind outside rattling *Wild Eyes'* rigging and
flogging her sails. Sometimes, as I scrambled fore and aft,
the boat rocked gunwale to gunwale, pitching me against the
bulkhead. I can't tell you how many times I dropped my flashlight and
had to scrabble to find it in the bottom of the boat, hoping it hadn't
fallen into water.

Over and over, wedged into the tiny pilot compartment, I followed
instructions from home:

. . . unplug one of the displays from pilot A and plug it into pilot
B . . .

. . . move multiple colored wires from A to B and back again (and
again and again . . .)

. . . move electronic components from the A box to the B box . . .

. . . switch the drive motor from the primary pilot to the backup . . .

. . . check all the fuses to see if they are still good . . .

. . . check the "mosfet," a particular transistor . . .

We tested dozens of different configurations. To see if the autopilot was working, I would have to run topside, set the rudder to port,
run below and push a button, run topside again, and set the rudder to
starboard, run below and push the button again, then activate the autopilot to see if it was steering the boat.

Again and again the answer was no.

Finally, Jeff taught me an old sailor's trick. Digging around in my sail locker, I found two long pieces of line. I went outside into the splashing darkness and tied them to the tiller, then ran them below to the brain box compartment. That way I could set the rudders and push the buttons without having to run back and forth.

As the hours dragged by with no progress, I was beginning to have trouble hearing what Jeff and Scott were saying. I was so tired, I was also beginning to have trouble remembering their instructions. I decided it would be a good idea if I could write down what they told me, turn off the phone to conserve battery power, then go try it. But when I got to the chart desk to look for paper, I found that my notebook was wet from my running back and forth through the cabin. The rest of my paper was packed away in the forward compartment. And the only pen I could find was a Sharpie.

Have skin, will travel.

I pulled up my sleeve, put the phone between my ear and shoulder, and as Jeff and Scott dictated instructions and schematics, I drew them on my arm. Then I would hang up the phone and go do whatever they told me to do.

I remember at one point, right around four in the morning my time, one of the guys asked, "Do you want to go get some rest? We can just finish this up in the morning."

I felt terrible for keeping them up so late. I mean, it was completely amazing what they were able to help me do in the blind from seven thousand miles away. Not only that, but they were so patient, and they never seemed one bit irritated that we had started this thing at 5:00 p.m. their time, and it was now almost 11:00 p.m.

But if I was going to fix this, I wanted to do it and get it over with. I didn't want to waste time, you know? I mean, the whole time I was working on the autopilots, I wasn't going anywhere. And while the weather was mild at the moment, at 57 degrees south, that wouldn't last for long.

Wild Eyes was just drifting. The guys and I had discussed me hand steering to the nearest land. If it came to that, I would, but I wasn't ready to give up yet. Still, every time I tried something and it didn't work, the awful possibility of having to stop was getting more and more real.

 Because he wasn't speaking directly with Abigail, and because Jeff and Scott didn't have time to translate technical updates to Marianne, Laurence had no way of knowing what, if any, progress was being made. But as the hours dragged on, it seemed to him less and less likely that Abby would be able to keep sailing, so he began to try to get out ahead of the problem. He had visions of having to tow *Wild Eyes* up the Beagle Channel, knowing all the while that repairing the autopilot at the End of the Earth would be like trying to fix it on the moon. They don't generally stock a lot of high-tech gear in either location.

Consulting by phone with John Selby, the man who had connected him with Ian, Laurence learned that Argentine customs was notoriously slow and difficult. The most reliable way to get the parts down, John said, would be to actually have someone pack them in ordinary suitcases and fly them down like luggage.

After talking with John, Laurence ran his hand around the five-day stubble that covered his chin, and turned to Ian, who stood at *Persimmon's* wheel. "I don't know, mate, but I think we might be pulling Abigail into Ushuaia."

 After Abby found her Sharpie, Jeff and Scott began giving their instructions in small bites—"Look at the diagram. Move the yellow, red, and green wires to the A box and keep track of which wires you're moving"—then the phone would go silent for fifteen minutes or so, until Abby got back on the line and reported her results. Sometimes fifteen minutes would stretch to thirty or more. Without Abby at the tiller, the men knew *Wild Eyes* was helpless, still about twenty miles from the westernmost islands of Chile, and now fifty miles from Cape Horn. Minutes seemed to stretch forever as they waited for her to call back. As they waited, Scott now at home and Jeff on his boat in Marina del Rey, they wondered if something terrible had happened.

By 2:00 a.m., Scott began having major doubts about whether the autopilots could be fixed. He remembers, at about the nine-and-a-half-hour mark, texting Jeff: "We're not going to solve this. Let's just point her toward Ushuaia, have her hand steer there, because we are not going to get this fixed."

Jeff doesn't remember what he texted back. But from the beginning, he had been running other scenarios in the back of his mind. What are the options? Abby was still in Chilean waters, and close enough to hand steer around Cape Horn and into the calmer bay to its north. Depending on winds and weather, the team might have to call the Chilean Coast Guard for help. And Laurence was somewhere south of Ushuaia; he could coordinate repairs.

Jeff contemplated another scenario: if they did get one autopilot working, should Abby continue on—to the Falkland Islands, or even to Cape Town, South Africa? Because if the single working autopilot failed, Abby would have to sit in the cockpit and hand steer through the inevitable storms that would thunder her way. It would be a miserable trip, wet and freezing. Abby would have to man the tiller nonstop for sixteen hours, then go below and grab four hours' sleep, letting *Wild Eyes* drift wherever she wished, even backward. Then she would have to hand steer for another sixteen hours, snatch more sleep, and on it would go all the way across the Atlantic Ocean. *Wild Eyes* herself was solid: the sails worked, the rudder worked. People had sailed for centuries without any technology at all. Plus, *Wild Eyes*' Scott Jutson design was virtually unsinkable.

Jeff asked himself a question: Is Abby tough enough?

The answer: Yes.

She would be cold and wet, but it wouldn't kill her . . .

"Wait a minute!" Jeff said.

As the troubleshooting marathon crawled into its tenth hour, he had a technical epiphany: "Why don't we take that little fuse Abby told us was good in box B and change it over to box A?"

"Okay," Scott said. "It's worth a try."

Jeff told Abby what to do, and she put down the phone.

 By the tenth hour, my clothes had been soaked through for what seemed like forever. My hair was plastered to my head. I'm sure if I'd had time to look in the mirror, I would have seen a dirty face smeared with grease from the hydraulic drives. My hands were so numb that I could barely manipulate the nail-clipper file I was using as a screwdriver.

When Jeff suggested switching just that one fuse, I didn't hold out much hope. It was a minor operation, so I didn't hang up, just went to the aft compartment, made the switch, and got back on the phone.

"It's done. I switched it."

"Okay, turn it on," Jeff said.

I pushed the power button on box A and was amazed when the display came alive.

 Abby popped up on the phone: "Pilot A is on."

"Wow," Jeff and Scott said almost simultaneously.

"Okay, do the setup," Jeff said, referring to the procedure of calibrating the rudder with the brain and drive.

The phone went silent again. Then Abby was back: "I think it's working!"

Like others who got to know her, Jeff and Scott had found that an exclamation point for Abby didn't mean the kind of jubilation or exuberance that it does for some people. When Abby got excited her voice notched only a tiny pitch higher—just a hint of joy that painted her voice a slightly brighter color.

Jeff also thought he detected a hint of amazement in her voice, and he didn't blame her. Over and over, the whole situation had reminded Jeff of the near-space-disaster involving Apollo 13. In the film, and in life, Houston-based experts performed engineering miracles to get astronauts Jim Lovell, Jack Swigert, and Fred Haise home on their lunar landing module after their main spacecraft went belly-up. During that mission, NASA had at least two experts for every system and subsystem—a NASA specialist and a manufacturer's rep on site or on call—who could diagnose a problem down to the micro-level. And still, when carbon dioxide levels reached dangerous levels and threatened to suffocate the three astronauts before they could make it home, those experts literally had to make a square peg fit in a round hole. They jury-rigged an air-scrubbing contraption out of a sock, a plastic bag, a flight manual cover, assorted odd objects, and lots of duct tape.

The lesson: in attempting great feats in small spaces with limited gear, there is simply no way to plan for every contingency.

Here were two technical experts sitting in Southern California and a young woman in a tiny boat drifting off Cape Horn in freezing waters in the middle of the night. Abby had certainly not traveled the distance of a moon shot. But as the Apollo 13 astronauts were not air-scrubber experts, neither was Abby the sailor a journeyman electronics technician. And, in using low-tech materials like line and a nail file to repair high-tech gear, assisted by technical experts thousands of miles away, she was very much in the same position as the astronauts on Apollo 13.

Jeff and Scott could hardly believe that after ten hours, this sixteen-year-old girl had actually ripped this electronic system apart a hundred different ways and used the pieces of two broken machines to cobble together a single working autopilot.

 After the display lit up and showed the autopilot up and running, I could hardly believe it. It was a huge relief, and my first thought was, *I don't have to stop!* But I was too exhausted to jump up and down—and if I had, I would have hit my head on the cabin roof anyway. I remember feeling pretty happy that I hadn't quit. I had never done anything even remotely close to fixing a piece of gear like that, and I had pushed through and got it done. And even though no one but my team and me knew what had just happened, I felt like I was finally beginning to prove myself to the critics.

More than half the people who had spoken up about my trip said I might make it a few weeks out at the most. And that I certainly wouldn't make it around Cape Horn. So they were all back there saying, "Oh, she can't do it." But I was doing it.

 When Laurence called Marianne to pass on his contingency plan, he was astonished when she said, "They fixed it! Abby got the autopilot working!"

Laurence thought it was an incredible testimony to the commitment and effort Jeff and Scott had put forth for his daughter. And for a father, it was also an incredible moment. When Abby was thirteen and popped up smiling from a raging sea, Laurence had thought she might have the tenacity for a solo-round. Now he was finding out for sure what she was really made of.

When a sailor overcomes crushing adversity, there's a massive sense of accomplishment. For ten wet, freezing, frustrating hours, she'd dealt calmly with a situation that even Jeff and Scott were describing in private Skype messages as likely hopeless. But Abby persevered and overcame. Laurence had always believed adults would be surprised at what young people can accomplish if given the chance, instead of being penned up like colts in a stable, unable to stretch their legs.

In constant communication with Commanders' Weather, Marianne had developed a good working relationship with Commanders' president, meteorologist Ken Campbell. Abby had had mild sea conditions during the autopilot ordeal, but that was unusual and wouldn't last for long. In a conversation with Ken just after Abby rounded Cape Horn, Marianne wondered aloud what kind of toll the stress of the ten-hour repair marathon might take on her daughter when combined with the steep seas and storms still ahead in the South Atlantic.

Ken had been routing sailors for thirty years in major international races and numerous solo-round campaigns. He told Marianne he'd seen grown men go through far less than Abby had before beginning to whine and complain and ask to be pulled off their boats.

"Abby's not even showing signs of quitting yet," Ken said. "She's nowhere near done."

CHAPTER 12
CLOSE CALL

CAPE HORN AND THE SOUTH ATLANTIC
MARCH–MAY 2010

 On March 31, I set my first record, becoming the youngest person ever to solo around Cape Horn! The bad news was, I was so exhausted from the ten-hour autopilot nightmare that I'd set my course and slept right through it. I guess it wouldn't have mattered if I'd been awake—I was fifty to sixty miles offshore when I went around and couldn't have seen the Cape anyway. But when I woke up, looked at my chart plotter, and saw that I'd made it, I was super excited.

The big bummer, though, was not being able to hook up with my dad. It would've been so cool if we could have connected. That way we could have kind of rounded the Horn together.

Ever since I left Cabo, Bill Bennett had been sending me cheerful e-mails to keep my spirits up, and after my ordeal with the autopilot, I was ready for some humor. On April 1, the day after I rounded Cape Horn, I found this note to me from my team posted on my blog:

ABBY,

AFTER MUCH LENGTHY DISCUSSION, TEAM ABBY HAS DECIDED THAT TO BE CERTAIN THAT EVERYONE IN THE OFFICIAL YACHTING WORLD FULLY ACCEPTS THE FACT THAT YOU TRULY SAILED AROUND THE WORLD SOLO, WE HAVE DECIDED YOU WILL NEED TO SAIL AROUND THE WORLD TWICE, JUST TO PROVE TO THEM THAT YOU INDEED ACTUALLY DID IT . . .

DURING THE DISCUSSION, THE SUBJECT OF PIRATES DID COME UP, WITH EVERYONE'S CONCERN THAT THERE IS A REAL DANGER THEY MIGHT STALK AND KIDNAP YOU FOR RANSOM SOMEWHERE DURING YOUR SECOND LAP . . . SO AS A SOLUTION, SCOTT HAS OFFERED TO PUT IN A CALL TO HIS FRIENDS . . . IN THE U.S. COAST GUARD . . .

BUT JUST IN CASE THE PIRATES SLIP BY THE COAST GUARD AND MANAGE TO KIDNAP YOU ANYWAY, WE HAVE STARTED A PAYPAL FUND TO RAISE RANSOM MONEY WE WILL USE TO BUY YOU BACK. JEFF REPORTS THAT SO FAR, HE HAS RAISED $38, WHICH WE ALL FEEL SHOULD BE PLENTY OF MONEY, WE HOPE.

LOVE, TEAM ABBY

That was my April Fool's Day greeting from my team, and I got a kick out of it when I finally read it on April 2. (So I guess the joke was on them.)

That was the same day I officially crossed into a new ocean, the South Atlantic. I saw land for the first time in two months: Staten Island—or *Isla de los Estados*, east of Tierra Del Fuego and Strait de Le Maire. I wished I could've stopped on Staten Island and visited the adorable penguins who live there and will walk right up to you! But I was on a nonstop, so that wouldn't have worked. Plus, after rounding the cape, it was really important for me to get north as quickly as possible because the Southern Ocean is notorious for icebergs.

When they sailed to Alaska, Jeff and Gail Casher had once made rum-and-cokes with ice from an iceberg. I definitely didn't want to get that close.

To get north quickly, Commanders' Weather recommended a route that would take me west of the Falkland Islands. In making my way past the Falklands, I was running into headwinds of about twenty knots. *Wild Eyes* didn't sail well close to the wind—or "close-hauled"—which is when the boat is pointing into the wind as closely as possible without stalling. So northing against the wind was a huge fight. And the farther north I sailed, the closer to the Falklands I got. I knew that once I passed them, I'd have to make a right turn and head east. But I was only about thirty miles from the northernmost islands by then, and I didn't want to turn them into what sailors called a "lee shore."

Technically, a lee shore is just the shore that the wind is blowing toward. But to sailors, a lee shore is one that is to the lee side of a vessel—a shore that a strong wind could wreck your boat on, especially if your boat doesn't sail well into the wind, like *Wild Eyes*. So I made a command decision: I had already spent long enough battling upwind, so I turned *Wild Eyes* south, passed underneath the Falklands, then hung a left, and headed deeper into the South Atlantic.

For the next several days, I had a nice swell running and surprisingly warm temperatures, up to sixty-three degrees. So warm I had to take my sweater off! I had winds from fifteen to twenty-five knots, which were great for generating power to store up for days when there wasn't any sun. When some people following my blog asked me how things were going, I realized I had a "new normal" in life: I'd lost my hairbrush (again), my boots were still wet, I hadn't caught any fish, and my schoolwork was . . . well, proceeding slowly. Still, I *was* learning a lot in the South Atlantic, like how a sudden drop in water temperature can mean "Iceberg Ahead," so I was watching my water temperature gauge and counting that as science, even if it wasn't from a book.

Then, just as I was getting in the groove of sailing along in the swells, the wind dropped almost to a dead calm. Just as bad, everything around me turned to gray. Gray water, gray clouds, and thick patches of gray fog. Except for the sound of water sloshing weakly against my boat, the world became quiet and weird, like being in another dimension. In sunny Southern California, I had loved cloudy weather, but now I realized it was because we hardly ever had any. Now I found it kind of depressing. Meanwhile, *Wild Eyes* was crawling along like a garden slug. It seemed like this ocean was taking *forever* to cross! I knew it was the second largest ocean on the planet and everything, but still.

 You know that saying, "Be careful what you wish for?" I had been wishing not to be so bored. I got my wish—and then some.

I was about fifteen hundred miles past the Falklands and it was night. The wind had picked up and I was reefed all the way down. Those lovely warm temperatures I had been enjoying were long gone and I was all bundled up against the cold. But as usual, my boots were drenched, so my feet were bare. Suddenly, I felt the wind kick up even more. My gauges showed gusts to fifty knots.

Now even the third reef wouldn't make my sail small enough. I knew I would have to take the whole mainsail down, which is a rough job in high winds because it's huge and hard to handle. I put my harness on, went topside, and clipped in to the jack lines that run from bow to stern.

It was pitch-black out and whitewater was crashing over the boat.

The wintry wind screamed across the deck, and I could tell it was now holding up near fifty knots. Imagine standing on the roof of a car that's driving down the freeway. That's how hard it was blowing. I let the mainsheet out some to spill air. As the mainsail flogged crazily in the racing wind, I had to climb all over the boom and do the monkey thing to try and get it down. But the way I was clipped in to the jacklines, my harness line didn't reach far enough for me to get the job done. So I unclipped it, wrapped it around the boom to shorten the line and clipped it back onto itself. Then I started working to get the sail down.

At that moment, a huge gust slammed into the mainsail like a train. The autopilot snapped into standby. *Wild Eyes* jibed and the boom began a wild swing. The boat heeled over to port as if a giant hand had smacked her down, and I tumbled over the top of the mainsail toward the water. Terror ripped through me as I was falling, falling, falling toward the sea. *Wild Eyes* was nearly mast down in the water when my harness line jerked me to a stop.

Now I was hanging there, my boat heeled over at least eighty degrees, still moving forward, but nearly on her side. Only the running backstay had kept the boom from swinging all the way to port, knocking me overboard, and holding me underwater.

Wild Eyes was almost perpendicular to the sea, her deck a vertical wall. The mainsail hung over me like a roof, and I was hanging from the boom by the safety line. The boat was still making way, rocking violently, dragging my legs through the water. Fear fluttered in my chest like bats, but I had to shut it down. I had to figure out what to do.

Pointing my legs toward the deck, I felt around with my bare feet until they found a stanchion on the low side of the boat. Putting both feet on it, I used my legs to pull myself toward the deck. Blindly, I felt over my head.

There! A handhold!

It was the handrail on the dome over the companionway. I grabbed on.

But I was still trapped.

From my position I couldn't reach the end of my safety line where I had tied in to the boom. Even if I could have, with all the G-force pushing me toward the water, the instant I unclipped, I would fall into the Atlantic, and *Wild Eyes* would sail away without me.

The wind wailed. Freezing waves broke against my body. Between waves, I was standing in the water, sometimes knee deep. I couldn't stay where I was. I had only one choice: I had to unclip the safety line from my harness.

It was a terrifying choice: do it or die . . . or maybe, do it *and* die. Once I unclipped the harness, there would be nothing tethering me to my boat. If a big wave came at the wrong moment, it would sweep me off into forty-eight-degree water, where I might last twenty minutes. Drowning quickly might be better.

But if I didn't unclip the line, there was no way I could crawl back aboard and right my boat. I had no choice. I had to do it. At that moment adrenaline and the will to live overpowered all my fear. I unclipped the black buckle from the harness.

Clinging to the handrail, I side-stepped aft along the gunwale. Rolling swells washed across me as I picked my way along, and the boat rolled with them. When I had to, I walked on the lifelines that stretched between the stanchions. They were not meant to hold a person, and they wobbled and flexed under my weight.

Finally, I was standing underneath the cockpit. With one hand I grabbed the stainless steel pole that held up my dodger. With the other, I grabbed the edge of the cockpit. Then, using every ounce of strength I had to climb up the deck, I pulled myself into the cockpit.

No time to break down now. Moving quickly, I grabbed the tiller. There was still enough rudder in the water for me to be able to steer. I put the boat back on course and reengaged the autopilot. *Wild Eyes* righted herself and began cutting through the freezing darkness.

Still I couldn't rest. I had to clip in again, and finish pulling down the main. Now *I* was on autopilot. In winds now steady at forty knots, the sail flogged and fought me, but I got it down.

Finally, the boat was in order. I unclipped, went below, and sat down at my chart desk. Slowly, my brain let me in on the fact that I had just come *this close* to dying. After that, it took me a couple of hours to stop shaking.

 By mid-April, my autopilots had begun acting crazy again. Since rounding Cape Horn, I had been down to just one working pilot, with spare parts for repairs. But there always seemed to be a new problem. On April 22, for example, I was fiddling around with it, trying a few different tricks that usually helped it behave a little better. But when I disengaged the autopilot and reset it, it didn't work at all! I could hear the engine trying to turn the rudder, but the tiller was completely loose. I could steer with my hand while the autopilot was engaged.

It was about this time that I started thinking what it would be like to hand steer across the rest of the Atlantic Ocean. Not a very nice thought. What I ended up doing was wiring the main autopilot hydraulic ram and engine to the backup autopilot brain box. And it worked!

With all the trouble I was having, my team back home had been gently listing the pros and cons of pulling into Cape Town, South Africa. They were leaving the decision up to me, but I was avoiding even the thought of it. I mean, there were other places beyond the African coast where I could stop if I had to. Australia, for example.

Plus, at that moment in my trip, I was on a roll, making way, *Wild Eyes'* bow cutting nicely through the sea. Yes, I'd had equipment failures and close calls, but I had overcome them all. I had been alone at sea for three months and I didn't want to stop.

Even as that spirit of adventure, of competing against the sea, dominated my emotions, troubling thoughts kept poking at my brain. Annoying thoughts, like, "The boat really *does* need some work" and "It's really not safe to be out here with the autopilots acting up all the time." Even though we'd been able to repair the autopilots several times, there seemed to be no rhyme or reason to their ups and downs. None of us was sure why it was working now, or why it had failed before.

So, as *Wild Eyes* sailed toward Africa, my brain and my heart were locked in a civil war. My heart wanted to keep going because putting in at Cape Town would end my nonstop trip. But my brain knew better: *If you don't stop, you'll have an entire ocean ahead of you, once you pass Cape Agulhas. If the autopilots flip out again, it's going to be pretty serious.*

Cape Agulhas ("Cape of Needles") is the rocky stretch of coastline at the southernmost point of the African continent. At its tip, there's a classic-looking lighthouse painted in red and white stripes, and a stone monument that marks the official divide between the Atlantic and Indian oceans. The seas off Cape Agulhas can churn up storms wicked enough to sink large ships. And beyond the cape, there's about a thousand miles of nothing.

In the tug-of-war between my brain and heart, my brain won out. It would be unsafe to keep going. My goal was to sail solo and nonstop around the world, not to die of stupidity.

As much as I hated to do it, I got on the phone with the guys and told them, "Yeah, I think I need to stop in Cape Town."

Later I found out that several members of Team Abby had thought that's exactly what I should do, but they weren't telling me, "Hey, you need to stop." They were saying, "Hey, your boat's kind of falling apart and it would be good if you stopped." They weren't going to make me; they trusted me to make the right decision.

It still tore me up to do it. It ached way down in my gut. Like a marathoner, I had found a "zone," and my heart was screaming at me to battle it out, to put up with the inconvenience and risk. Also, I had begun to let the public pressure mess with my head. My trip had been hyped as "solo, nonstop, and unassisted."

I mean, originally I thought, *Who cares what happens? If I have to stop, it just adds to the adventure, to the sights I get to see, the people I get to meet.* But now I felt like the whole world was looking at me, and I had begun to care too much what the critics would say. I was in my old mode of trying to make everybody happy, trying to answer everyone's questions.

But my head, now ten thousand miles wiser, was telling me that to keep going wasn't the right thing to do.

There will be people, I thought, *who will say that if I was a "real" sailor, I would've stuck it out and hand steered the rest of the way. But I've decided to stop, and they'll just have to get over it.*

Finally, I made the announcement on my blog. "It would be foolish and irresponsible for me to keep going with my equipment not working well . . ." I wrote. "I know that some people will look on my trip as a failure because of this, and there really isn't anything I can do about that. When you're surrounded by critics, it can be hard to remember your own goals and expectations; you start to judge yourself by what other people are saying."

My whole trip came from a dream, I wrote, a dream to sail around the world: "And that is what I'm doing—youngest or not, nonstop or stopping."

Two days before pulling into Cape Town was a red-letter day: I had spent one hundred days alone at sea. I spent most of that day sitting outside in the sun and wind and thinking about all that had happened in the journey that had so far taken me halfway around the world: Raging storms, dead calms, endless days and nights working to keep my equipment running. The big moments, like rounding Cape Horn. I looked out across the water, the sun dancing and sparkling on the crests, and thought, *I'm happy out here.*

There had been great times and terrifying times, and as weird as it sounds, I loved everything about it. I thought how strange it was going to be to see people again. To walk on dry land, sleep in a dry bed. I wished it didn't have to happen. Losing the nonstop record wasn't such a big deal after having done what I'd done. It was just being out there with the sea and sky that seemed to change like a kaleidoscope, like God repainting my surroundings every day.

I loved it. I wished there was a way to spend the rest of my life out there.

Zac had told me that going into port can be hard. It can be even harder to leave, Zac said, hard to get back into the rhythm and routine of life at sea.

On April 24, I received an encouraging note from Bill:

ABBY,

YOU HAVE MADE A TOUGH DECISION, BUT A GOOD ONE. I KNOW YOU WERE DISAPPOINTED WHEN YOU FINALLY CAME TO THE CONCLUSION THAT YOU WOULD HAVE TO STOP, BUT NOW I'M SURE YOU WILL FEEL SAFER AND MORE COMFORTABLE WITH PROPERLY WORK-ING SYSTEMS ON *WILD EYES*. MAYBE THE TITLE OF YOUR BOOK SHOULD BE "AROUND THE WORLD WITH SHARPIES, CHEWING GUM, AND STRING." THAT'S A BAD JOKE, SORRY, BUT REALLY I AM INCREDIBLY IMPRESSED WITH YOUR ABILITY TO CONTINUALLY ASSESS AND REPAIR MAJOR THINGS ON THE BOAT. BRAVO TO YOU FOR THAT.

Bill went on to explain that he had a friend, Jannie van Wyck, who owned a ranch in the country outside of Cape Town. Jannie and his wife had offered to host me, my dad, and any teammates who were able to make the trip to work on the boat.

A ranch in South Africa? That sounded pretty cool. After reading

Bill's e-mail, I went topside, planted myself in the cockpit, and enjoyed the sunshine. As *Wild Eyes'* bow sliced through the glistening water, I thought you could make a pretty good argument that it is a little bit of a waste to sail around the entire world and yet not actually get to see any of it.

CHAPTER 13

TUNE-UP AND REFIT

CAPE TOWN, SOUTH AFRICA
MAY 2010

 On May 5, five miles out from Cape Town, I was soaked, freezing, and miserable. A frigid wind whipped across *Wild Eyes*' deck. Even though I had tried very hard to find the silver linings, in the end my heart refused to cooperate. I wasn't very happy that my nonstop trip was ending that day. On top of all that, I was swamped in fog so thick it seemed like a solid object, like sailing through a giant block of cotton. I knew there were huge ships headed in and out of port, less than half a mile from me. That's because the AIS was blasting my eardrums like an air raid siren every five or ten seconds. I was not happy.

Then, suddenly, as if God decided to give me a break, the wind died down and the fog began to clear. As soon as I decided it was safe, I went below and switched off the AIS. When I went topside again, a dolphin darted through the water and poked his head up to say hi. Then he arced through the water again and again. As I made my way into the harbor, the dolphin didn't seem to have any intention of leaving. He stayed with me kind of like he was guiding me, and that cheered me up a little.

 After an eighteen-hour flight from Los Angeles through New York and Johannesburg to Cape Town, Laurence and Scott joined Jannie van Wyck on an inflatable rib boat and sped seaward in Cape Town harbor, battling an eight-foot swell. The boat flew up the front sides of the waves, got briefly airborne, then splashed down in the troughs, spray flying. The wet, pounding trip reminded Scott of time he'd spent aboard Boston whalers when he was thirteen and fourteen years old.

For Jannie van Wyck, heading out to meet *Wild Eyes* was a historic moment. His parents were filmmakers who had been involved in making *Dove*, the movie about Robin Lee Graham, the teenage solo-rounder who had inspired Abby and Zac since they were young. The van Wycks bought one of the "Doves" used in the film and sailed it for years afterward.

Laurence, meanwhile, held on during the wet, bumpy ride, and was unusually quiet. Not being able to see Abby round Cape Horn had been a bitter disappointment for him. After the travel, the expense, the coordination, and the generous help of John Selby, Ian Upsall, and his crew, Laurence felt he had failed his daughter. Still, the trip to Ushuaia had a sweet side. While he was disappointed in himself, he had felt his soul smiling for Abby, whispering, *She's doing it! She's pulling it off against the odds and against the mechanical breakdowns. She's proving her mettle.*

As the rib boat smashed through the swells, Laurence began

looking for his daughter again. There weren't many sailboats braving the rough harbor, but two or three times a sail did emerge from the thick mist and Laurence's heart soared. But none of them was Abby.

Soon the fog began to lift. Laurence had a camera with him and began using the zoom lens to try and spot *Wild Eyes*.

There!

The tip of her sail peeked up from a trough, then *Wild Eyes* popped up into full view, sails full of wind. Through the zoom lens, Laurence could see Abby on deck. He was amazed: she looked to him as if she'd just been on a weekend sail, instead of more than a hundred days at sea. Laurence's heart raced as the boats drew near each other. He could see the exact moment when Abby caught sight of him. She raised her arm in a happy wave.

Here was his sixteen-year-old daughter after ten thousand miles at sea!

Laurence will never forget the moment the boats came side by side, and Abby smiled and caught his eye—a deep, special moment between father and daughter, a thousand words exchanged without speaking one.

 I was so happy to see my dad! I was sad when we weren't able to connect at Cape Horn and share that achievement together. But now, here he was, and it felt like a little bit of home.

Then I had a downer moment. I saw a big powerboat motoring toward me. I had learned to spot reporters by then and from all the gear these people were carrying, I could tell this boat was packed with them. My heart started racing and my nerves tingled with fear. Then I got a grip and had to laugh at myself a little. I'd been halfway around the world, nearly drowned, had spent the previous nights dodging many large freighters in the Cape Town shipping lanes, and now this little sixty-foot powerboat with a few reporters onboard was scaring me! Then as the powerboat rumbled closer, I saw a familiar face: my brother Zac grinning and waving at me.

It was a good thing Dad and Scott showed up in the rib boat because right then, my engine started coughing black smoke and died a sudden death right there in the channel. At first I thought, *Wow, I guess I made the right decision, stopping in Cape Town*. It later turned out that a nasty piece of kelp as thick as rawhide had wrapped itself around my propeller and fouled it. No problem, though, we just tied *Wild Eyes* to the rib boat, and they pulled me the rest of the way in.

There's a swing bridge that crosses the Cape Town harbor, and the port workers open it for boats to pull into the marina. I was so surprised to see people lining the concrete embankments on both sides of the bridge, yelling and waving and clapping, cheering me as I was being towed through the channel.

Also, there was this 120-foot sailboat called *Pink Gin* that I had e-mailed back and forth with a few times on my way into Cape Town. They happened to arrive in the harbor just before me, and all my e-mail friends were now standing on deck in person, waving and cheering as I went by. I hadn't expected well-wishers in Cabo, and now here were more of them in Cape Town. It was neat to think that people in different countries were following and supporting my trip.

Then came the strangest surprise of all. When we pulled *Wild Eyes* into a slip and I got off the boat, there was a man standing there holding a silver tray. On it were a big, juicy-looking cheeseburger and a huge pile of French fries. The man holding it was Andrew Rosettensteinlast, the assistant manager of Cape Grace, a five-star hotel on the Victoria and Albert Marina. After one hundred days of dehydrated space noodles, that burger and fries was the most awesome plate of food I had ever seen! But I was too busy talking to reporters to even take a bite!

The next day, Scott and Laurence surveyed *Wild Eyes* and took stock of everything that needed to be replaced or repaired. Scott's cast had been removed by then, and he had full use of his hand. No more metal pins in his fingers, but he did still have those six titanium plates in his face.

Jannie van Wyck's business was to supply filmmakers working in his region. He gave Scott and Laurence use of his warehouse as a base of operations.

Because the open ocean is such a harsh environment, competitors in circumnavigation races, such as the Velux 5 Oceans Race, must pull into ports and have their boats and systems tweaked, overhauled, or replaced before continuing the next leg of the race. Of all those who begin circumnavigation races, only an estimated 60 percent complete them, either because their boats break up at sea or, once in port, are beyond repair.

In *Wild Eyes*' case, Scott and Laurence had decided on a near overhaul. Working twelve to sixteen hours a day for a little more than two weeks, Scott, Laurence, and Zac installed two new wind generators, two new alternators, waterproof voltmeters, LED lighting, and new, upgraded autopilots donated by the manufacturer of Abby's original autopilots. The upgrade included two new brain boxes. Each autopilot also had two new remotes, one below and one in the cockpit, hardwired into the system, instead of plugged in. The manufacturer provided new compasses, as well, so that the only components remaining from the original system were the drive units and sensors in the aft compartment.

Abby hadn't been the best housekeeper in the world, so Scott and Zac helped her clean up the cabin and reorganize and stow all her gear. Laurence spent a lot of time running around to various shops collecting parts for Scott. He had been to Cape Town during Zac's sail and knew the drill—in Cape Town, you can't buy everything in one shop, as in the U.S.

"It's like someone sells a screw in one shop, a nut for the screw in another shop, and a washer for the screw in another," he explained to Scott one day. Laurence found it very inefficient and frustrating because he had learned from Zac's sail that running around all over the city would eat up the precious time they had to fix Abby's boat before her Southern Ocean weather window closed for good.

 Just like with Cabo, the thing I remember about Cape Town the most is the people. There was Jannie, the friend of Bill Bennett's who was in the film business. My mom and dad had met Jannie and his wife, Tracy, while they were in Los Angeles a few months prior. Dad and I stayed with the van Wycks. I had a great time getting to know their children James, 8, and Anna, 4, as well as Sisandra and Sinazo, two African girls Jannie had informally adopted after their father died. Spending time with Jannie and Tracy and their kids and two dogs reminded me a lot of my own busy, bustling home. It was a great experience staying at their house and getting to know them all.

I think the reason I remember the people more than anything about the country itself was that I had been alone at sea for more than three months since setting sail from Cabo. When I left Marina del Rey, I was not much of a people person. I think that's why a lot of sailors sail—just to be out with the sun and salt and sea air, away from all the rushing around and yakking. But when I pulled into Cape Town, something inside me had changed. I thought people were the greatest thing *ever*. I mean, it didn't matter *who* they were, I was just so happy to see them!

On May 16, while I was still in Cape Town, Jessica Watson pulled into Sydney, Australia. That meant she became the youngest person to sail solo, nonstop and unassisted around the world—the record I'd been hoping to break. That was rough.

I thought of all the what-ifs: What if I had used different autopilots? What if my wind generators had worked the whole time? What if I had just gone for it, instead of stopping in Cape Town?

I think Jessica's a great person and I thought her achievement was amazing. But that didn't take away the pain of watching somebody else live the dream I'd had since I was a young girl. When Jessica crossed her finish line, I congratulated her on my blog and I really meant it. I wrote:

> Before I go into everything we've done today, I'd just like to send a BIG congratulations to Jessica Watson! She has done an absolutely amazing thing and while, to be perfectly honest, I am a little envious, she deserves the record. She sailed around the world, alone, nonstop and unassisted. I know how difficult that is to achieve.

 Work continued on *Wild Eyes* and Commanders' Weather had given Abby the green light to continue. Rather than have her sail deep in the Southern Ocean, where winds would be steadier but significantly stronger, Abby would sail conservatively between 38 and 42 South. She would have to contend with flukier winds, but would be able to avoid heavier ones by sailing up in more northern latitudes.

A few days before Abby's scheduled launch from Cape Town, she and Laurence sat together at a pub at the top of the dock, having a bite to eat. Laurence had been planning how he was going to broach a sensitive subject with Abby. He believed people can get so wrapped up in the pressure and excitement of a thing that they sometimes need a reality check, or even an escape hatch. Most of what we do in life isn't the be-all and end-all, but we make it that, Laurence felt. We make it so important that we're willing to sacrifice almost anything for it.

Collecting his thoughts, Laurence grew still and serious. "You know, Abigail, you don't have to do this," he said. "Forget about the record and the critics and what anyone says. You can get on a plane with Zac and me and leave here right now. You don't have to finish now. You can leave *Wild Eyes* here, come home with me, and finish in the spring."

Abby sat quietly for a moment and then looked her father in the eye. "I know what my boat can do, and I know what I can do, and I want to keep going."

The protective father inside him wanted to wrap his daughter in a hug right then and not let go until she was on a plane with him back to L.A. But there was a bigger part of him that knew Abby was a world-class sailor, and that she needed to make the decision.

So on the outside, Laurence smiled and said, "As long as you're happy out there and you're confident, that's good with me."

But not quite good enough. To be sure Abby wasn't just giving the answer she thought her father would want to hear, Laurence asked Scott to have the same conversation with her. After waiting a couple of days, Scott did, and Abby's answer was the same: "I want to keep going."

No one, including Laurence, would find out until long after her trip was over that Jeff Casher had pulled Abby aside in Marina del Rey. "You know it's been in the papers and on the news that your father's pressuring you to go. Is that true?"

"No," Abby said. "I want to go."

Then in Cabo San Lucas, Jeff had checked in with Abby again. "I can make this go away right now," he told her. "No one will ever know that it was you who decided you didn't want to go."

Her response was instant, confident, and unhesitating, Jeff remembers. "No," she said. "I really want to go."

 On May 21, *Wild Eyes* and I made it back out to sea. Getting out of Cape Town was looking pretty iffy there for a little while. The bascule bridge was broken and they had engineers working hard to fix it. In the end, though, they raised one half of the bridge by hand, so I would have just enough room to squeeze through without leaving my mast behind. I thought that was so great of them. In fact, everyone at the marina bent over backward to get me out on schedule.

It was sunny and gorgeous the day I set sail from Cape Town. I turned up the stereo real loud and spent the whole day on deck working, just keeping busy, pulling out sails, going through my boat, organizing everything. It took a few nights to pick my way out through the local shipping traffic. But once I was back on the open ocean, my autopilots worked perfectly and *Wild Eyes* raced over the heavy seas in nearly full sail.

At first I was happy to be back at sea; I had really missed it. But just as Zac had predicted, setting sail again was easier on my body than my heart. It was weird, because *Wild Eyes* was cutting through the sea faster than ever before. But I was missing people a lot more. Also, it wasn't a nice, gradual easing into life at sea, the way it was in the calmer, warmer waters off of Mexico. Instead, this was *slamming* back into life at sea.

After leaving Cape Town, I found that I wasn't enjoying some of the things that had kept me going during the first half of my voyage. Before Cape Town, when I was feeling down or frustrated, I could always go topside, sit on deck, and let the salty wind carry my blues away. It was a sure-fire cure, even when I was wet and cold and things were breaking down. Back then, even on bad days I had always found something to be happy about. But it wasn't like that anymore. Sailing was becoming more like work.

After a couple of days out, though, I started enjoying the new auto-pilot and the fact that I could keep way more sail up without worrying about the pilot going into standby. On May 23, I was making twelve to fifteen knots, so that was pretty fun. The same day, sailing two hundred miles offshore, I passed under Cape Agulhas, which is the southernmost tip of Africa—not Cape of Good Hope.

Cape Agulhas marked my passage into the Indian Ocean. I was

really excited about entering my third ocean—my fourth if you count the Southern Ocean. *Wild Eyes* and I had made it out of the Pacific, through the Southern Ocean, and across the Atlantic. After the Indian, we only had to cross the normally peaceful Pacific to complete the circle and make it home.

CHAPTER 14

GOING UP THE MAST

THE INDIAN OCEAN
MAY 2010

COMMANDERS' WEATHER

LAST POSITION:
    40 21S/22 40E AT 1415 UTC WED, MAY 26
PREPARED:
    1530 UTC WEDNESDAY, MAY 26, 2010

SUMMARY: WILL BE STRONGER N-NW TO N WINDS THRU THU,
WHICH WILL BE OK FOR CONTINUING TO THE E OR EVEN HEAD-
ING E-SE, BUT IF HEADING BACK, THEN NEED TO WAIT UNTIL
THE S WINDS DEVELOP BEHIND THIS NEXT COLD FRONT, WHICH
PUSHES THRU BETWEEN 00 AND 06 UTC FRI . . .

 The forecast I read that day showed a high-pressure system, or fairly calm weather, located south of 40S and east of 30E, with the next cold front still well to my west near 8-9E. But as the cold front headed east, Commanders' Weather said that I should expect shifting winds with increasing speed—twenty to thirty knots on Thursday, and by Friday, squalls containing wind gusts from forty to forty-five knots.

The forecast was dead-on accurate. After the high-pressure system passed, the cold fronts came hard and fast, bringing storm after storm. My Thrane & Thrane was down for some reason, so I couldn't get online and update my blog or check e-mail. E-mail had always been my way of communicating with my friends. So now, at the exact time I had started appreciating being around people more than ever before in my life, I was not only geographically alone—I was *alone* alone.

On May 27, still sailing below South Africa, I knew I was headed into even heavier weather. Already the winds were getting colder and beginning to howl, so it was time to reef in. Outside, there was no moon, and cloud cover blotted out the stars. In the thick darkness, I tried to pull down the main, but it wouldn't come down. Between the wind gauge below and the Commanders' Weather forecast, I knew I would be hitting winds of thirty to thirty-five knots, too much wind for the amount of sail I had up. That means bad things can happen. Your sail can tear suddenly. Or a sudden gust across the beam can knock your boat down. In waters of about fifty degrees, I didn't want that again.

Already, the wind howled past my ears, snaking down my collar and up my sleeves, so cold it felt like it was carrying frost with it. My hands were numb to my wrists. I needed either to get the sail down or heave to and ride it out.

I tried doing all sorts of stuff to lower the sail. I turned into the wind and let the waves crash over the bow while I tried to take the tension out of the sail and let it go slack. I tried hoisting the sail higher, then letting it come down—kind of the way you might when Venetian blinds get stuck. But nothing worked. I decided something must be holding the sail fast.

Standing at the bottom of the mast, with the deck rolling and pitching underneath me, I looked as far up the sail as I could see, but it was too dark to see much. You have to imagine the blackest black. It was like being in a pitching sea of tar with a cast iron lid on top.

I went below and grabbed a flashlight, then went back topside again and shined it upward. By the time the light punched through the darkness up the fifty-foot mast, the end of the beam was pretty weak. But I was able to just make out a little black line leading from the top of the main sail to one of the top spreaders—horizontal supports for the mast.

The line I was seeing was one that my rigger had put on the sail to help me pull down the main while still standing on the deck. I wasn't tall enough to reach the top of the main while standing on the deck, so Alan Blunt, the rigger, had attached this line. It had worked perfectly for my entire trip. Now, in the dim light at the top of the mast, I could see that the line had wrapped itself around one of the bolts that attached the spreaders to the mast.

Not good, I thought. *In fact, really bad.*

Because it meant I might have to go up the mast.

Going up the mast is one of the most dangerous things you can do as a solo sailor. During Zac's campaign, while he was sailing west from St. Helena in the Southern Atlantic toward Grenada, his friend Nick was sailing south toward Africa. Zac later heard that Nick's boat was found with nobody aboard and with the empty bosun's chair attached at mid-mast.

I had gone up the mast many times, in port and at sea. But even when tied to a dock, there had been several times when I'd hitched up my bosun's chair, hoisted myself up, but couldn't get back down again. It took only a slight breeze to tangle the lines below, and I was stuck up the mast and had to get someone to untangle the lines so I could lower myself to the deck again.

And those times, I was tied up in a boat slip in water as calm as a bathtub. Now I was in thirty-five-knot winds facing the prospect of going up. I would have to hook up a pulley to the halyard and sit in a sling-style seat. Of course, it would take two hands to keep tension on the lines that I was using to pull myself up, so I'd somehow have to keep shimmying up the freezing wet mast with my legs, avoiding obstacles like spreaders, radar antenna, and shrouds. And you can't let go of the line to avoid an obstacle or you'll plunge to the deck like a falling rock.

I was definitely worried. I weighed my options. One was to go hove to and wait for things to calm down a bit. Another was to try to make it into a port where it was calm. Mossel Bay or Port Elizabeth, maybe. But going into port now was not a real option because in the building conditions with so much sail up, I would risk a knockdown. Heaving to would be hard on the boat and on me with the boat being bashed by huge seas. On the other hand, if I did, *Wild Eyes* would not be over-powered with so much sail up.

I lined up my bosun's chair, my helmet, and a knife to cut the tangled line. Then I sat down at the chart desk and called home. Remembering what had happened to Nick, I wanted to run things past the team before I made a final decision.

 Abby's phone call triggered a flurry of conferences ashore. The dangers of going up the mast at sea were legendary. Laurence immediately called Rob Jordan, a family friend who had completed several circumnavigations and had tons of solo experience.

The terrifying physics of going up-mast in heavy seas are inescap-able. When you're standing on deck at sea level, you can feel the boat rocking and compensate for it with your own body movement. But at the top of the mast, the rocking at sea level translates into a twenty- to thirty-foot arc through the air. In addition, the physics of motion cause the top of the mast to careen back and forth through the air at many times the speed of the mast at deck level. Because of this, a sailor suspended up-mast from a block-and-pulley system is generally not strong enough to hold onto the mast and is flung away, like a child on a swing set. Team Abby knew that even if Abby were only halfway up her fifty-foot mast and couldn't hold on, she'd be flung out into the freezing dark, twenty-five feet over the roaring sea—more than two boat-widths away from *Wild Eyes*' hull. Worse, the mast would then tilt in the other direction, accelerating Abby's arc back to the boat. If she didn't hit the mast at high speed, she'd go swinging out to the opposite side.

That would be the good news. The more times she missed, the faster she'd be traveling when she finally slammed into the mast. And it wasn't *if* she hit the mast; it was *when*. At that point, Abby would be either severely injured or dead.

But even if she suffered only a broken arm, she would still be the only person aboard. How would she get herself down? Cut the rope, plunge five stories, and hope not only to hit a rolling deck just eleven feet wide but also to survive the fall?

As Abby lay sleepless aboard *Wild Eyes*, Laurence and Rob hunkered down to sort through potential solutions. If Abby had to go up-mast, they needed to do two things. One, try to minimize the chance of her swinging out over the Indian Ocean; and two, ensure she had a safety system in place, a second set of lines.

Abby's primary system was a block-and-tackle pulley. It featured an automatic latch that locked in and stabilized her position whenever she stopped her movement up or down the mast. Before her departure, Abby had learned how to rig a second single line with a fat knot that slid up and down like a seat. That way, if the primary system tangled or failed, she could cut herself loose and slide down the secondary line. But Team Abby was worried about that option because she hadn't practiced it a lot, and certainly not in high winds and pitching seas.

The team also spent a lot of time weighing options on the best place for her to try and make her ascent. To minimize the possibility of a wild and dangerous swing ride, she could, they thought, attach herself to some other part of the boat. One possibility was to use a rope to anchor herself to the staysail on the front of the boat. The staysail rigging reached high enough up the mast that Abby could probably reach the tangled line. On the other hand, she'd have to hang from the block-and-tackle face up, as in one of those challenge courses where a line stretches over a canyon and people pull themselves across hand over hand. Except that Abby would be pulling herself *up*. In wicked winds.

While this solution would reduce the risk of a collision with the pitching mast, there was another problem: exhaustion. Adrenaline can sometimes super-charge people so that they can cope under severe duress (like those stories of people lifting an automobile to save a trapped child). But that kind of strength lasts only moments. Abby would have to be strong a lot longer than that. In the end, the team settled on a different fix. Abby would rig up the second line—the safety line with the knot in it—going up the back side of the mast.

 With the team working on a solution ashore, I went topside to try a few things Jeff had suggested might free the sail. The wind swept across *Wild Eyes'* beam as cold as invisible snow, and seawater splashed in over the deck. I wanted to unstick this line somehow, some way, because I definitely did not want to go up the mast. I was especially certain of this after I experimented with clipping the pulley onto the halyard for a test run. Shrieking like a pack of maniacs, the wind whipped the pulley system all over the place. As I tugged the line to see if I could raise it up the mast, it got stuck every place it could get stuck—and so bad that I couldn't get it unstuck.

Feeling frustration start to build in my chest, I squashed it like a cockroach before it could turn to fear. I sat down in my cockpit, which by now was full of water and swirling like a freezing Jacuzzi. I needed to think things through. I needed to be smart about this. This wasn't an emergency, at least not yet. Yeah, I'd have to stop for the night, but that wouldn't be the end of the world.

 Back in Thousand Oaks, hours flew by like minutes for Marianne. While Jeff, Rob, and Laurence had been working on technical solutions, Marianne had e-mailed a prayer request:

URGENT PRAYER REQUEST:

PLEASE PRAY FOR ABBY SUNDERLAND TONIGHT. SHE LEFT CAPE TOWN, SOUTH AFRICA, ON FRIDAY AND SHE HAS BEEN MAKING GREAT TIME. UNFORTUNATELY, A ROPE THAT IS ATTACHED TO HER MAINSAIL HAS TANGLED ITSELF AROUND HER TOPMOST SPREADERS (HORIZONTAL BAR COMING OFF OF THE MAST). SHE CANNOT GET HER MAINSAIL DOWN AND SHE CANNOT FREE THE LINE WITH-OUT GOING UP THE MAST. SHE HAD TO STALL HER BOAT OUT BY TURNING INTO THE WIND AS SHE HAD TOO MUCH WIND ON HER HUGE MAINSAIL AND THE BOAT COULD NOT STEER ITSELF. IT IS NIGHTTIME WHERE SHE IS BUT WHEN DAYLIGHT COMES SHE WILL HAVE TO CLIMB THE MAST AND FREE THE LINE. ABBY HAS BEEN UP THE MAST MANY TIMES AND HAS BEEN UP THE MAST AT SEA BUT NEVER IN THE CONDITIONS THAT SHE WILL HAVE TO GO UP IN TOMORROW.

AFTER PRAYER DURING ZAC'S TRIP, MANY MIRACU-LOUS WEATHER CHANGES TOOK PLACE! SO WE ARE ASKING THAT YOU WOULD PRAY FOR ABBY. (IT WILL BE DAYLIGHT THERE AROUND 9 PM HERE AND SHE WILL LIKELY GO UP BETWEEN OUR 9 PM TO 12 AM.) PLEASE PRAY THAT

THE WIND AND SEAS WOULD BE CALM ENOUGH FOR HER
TO SAFELY GET UP THE MAST, FREE THE LINE AND GET
BACK DOWN.

    WE WILL SEND OUT AN UPDATE AS SOON AS WE HAVE
ANY NEWS.

    MANY THANKS,

    THE SUNDERLANDS

Marianne initially sent the e-mail out to a huge list of friends and supporters, who in turn passed it literally around the world. Then, the entire team waited . . . and waited . . . and waited . . . for Abby to check back in. While they waited, Laurence and Marianne discussed something they knew their daughter wouldn't like: If she couldn't get the main down and had to pull into port so soon after leaving Cape Town, maybe that was God's way of saying, "That's enough."

Maybe it was time to pull her in for good.

With Abby's sail stuck high in dark and violent seas, Marianne's stomach churned. She prayed for God's hand to be on her daughter, and for the phone to ring.

Finally, it did.

"I thought something terrible had happened!" Marianne couldn't help saying when she finally heard Abby's voice across the miles. Marianne put the phone on speaker.

"No, I was just out trying some things," Abby said. "But I've decided to go hove to and ride it out for the night."

"I think that's the best thing, Abby," Laurence said. "We're talking to Commanders' to see where there might be some lighter conditions for you to go up the mast."

Jeff and Rob popped up on the bridge and filled Abby in on what they thought the safest procedure would be for going up. And they agreed with her that the smart play was to wait until morning.

Disappointed, but convinced it was the right thing to do, I went hove to. That meant turning *Wild Eyes* into the wind and back-winding the main sail. That way I wasn't making any headway and the autopilots wouldn't be overpowered by the rising winds. I was exhausted and would've traded all the chocolate on my boat to be able to pull down my bed and get a good night's sleep. But with *Wild Eyes* now at the mercy of the sea, I could hear the waves bashing over her bow and roaring across the deck. Inside, the cabin pitched and heaved. I spent the night sitting at the chart desk—soaked, freezing, and miserable.

When morning came the sun was out, but things were worse. During the night, the slamming sea had snapped the lines that attached my bowsprit to the boat. The bowsprit is a spar, or pole, that extends from the bow. Mine was white with a smiley face painted on the end. Now it hung from the bow, still secured to the boat by a single line near the waterline. Looking down, I could see the smiley face thrashing around in the churning water.

At that point, I probably cursed. With the prospect of having to go up the mast still looming in my mind, I had enough to deal with. But I couldn't leave the bowsprit slamming around in the water or it might damage my hull. I'd have to either haul it aboard or cut it free.

Grabbing my gaff pole from the cockpit, I crawled out to the very tip of *Wild Eyes'* bow and used the pole to grab the remaining bowsprit line. But with the heavy seas tossing my boat around like a toy, I wasn't able to stand up and haul the bowsprit aboard. Even if I cut it free, I would have to let it go. I pulled out my knife and began trying to cut through the line.

Wild Eyes was now slamming not only *into* waves but *through* them. Each time a wall of water raced over the bow, I had to let go of the line to keep from being washed overboard. So then I had to grab the gaff pole, fish the line from the water, and start over again. For more than an hour, I sat there soaked through and sawing, seawater pouring across my head.

Sometimes a smaller wave would wash over me and even though I didn't lose the line, it would rattle my hands and I'd cut myself with the knife.

I tried to look at the bright side—literally: at least it was light out. At least I wasn't having to try to do this in the dark. Still, by the time I sawed through the final line and watched the bowsprit sink into the deep, my hands were bleeding all over.

Well, I thought, *at least they're so numb I can't feel it.*

I went below and tried to dry out a little before calling home. The whole team was on the bridge, and we talked again about the plan Jeff, Rob, and Dad had come up with for going up-mast. Sailing into a port was out because the forecast showed I'd hit another monster storm before I could reach it. But Commanders' was reporting a high-pressure system about a hundred miles away—a patch of the planet with light winds and friendlier seas.

"We think you should make your way there, Abigail," my dad said. "Better chance of making it up and down the mast safely if you're in light winds."

I knew it was the right thing to do, but I still didn't like it. Sailing *toward* light winds was something I'd never done in my life. It would be like an Indy 500 driver having to make yet another pit stop. But like my pit stop in Cape Town, it was the wise thing to do. So I spent most of that day sailing toward a place I didn't want to go.

The next morning when I called home again, Mom got on the line. "Look, Ab, we've been talking. If you can't get the mainsail down, you're going to have to pull in somewhere."

I can't remember what I said to her, but I do remember what I was thinking: *Yep, okay, Mom. Sure. That's gonna happen.*

What I was going to do, I had decided, was hang up, go up the mast and take care of the problem. While I still had my mom on the phone, I went topside to see what the weather was doing. Suddenly, up in the air, a dark shape caught my eye. It was some kind of seabird and as I watched it fly right over my mast, a burst of joy filled my chest.

"Hey, Mom, hang on a sec," I said, and put the phone down. Peering up-mast in sunny skies, I could see the little line that had been knotted around the spreader.

It wasn't tangled anymore.

Somehow, miraculously, in the flailing wind, it had untangled itself. I reached up and let the main halyard go, and the mainsail came down, smooth as silk.

I picked up the phone and nearly shouted with happiness: "Mom, it's not stuck anymore!"

"What? How?"

"I don't know!" I said, laughing and happy for the first time in three days. "The little line that was tangled just untangled itself or something. I just pulled the halyard and the whole sail came right down!"

"Do you know how many people around the world were praying for you?" Mom said. I could hear the joy and amazement in her voice. "That's answered prayer!"

After I hung up, the first thing I did was cut that line off the mainsail. Then I hoisted the main again and got back on course.

I've thought a lot about how that line got free during a wind-whipped night in heavy seas. Things that are impossibly tangled in chaotic winds don't usually untangle themselves—they get worse. And because going up the mast is pretty much a death-defying act, my parents *had* asked hundreds of people around the world to pray. I knew Zac still chalked up a lot of the jams he had escaped to answered prayer. It might sound corny or overly religious, or whatever, but maybe God really did send an angel to untangle the line.

 After my little mainsail miracle, the weather over the next few days grew amazingly quiet. The winds slowed to the low teens and the seas flattened out a bit too. I loved lots of wind and big seas, but the weather gave me a chance to get some work done on the boat. Most of my equipment was working, including both autopilots. It was such a relief to have reliable autopilots. Since leaving Cape Town, there were some days that I racked up more than two hundred miles. My goal was two-hundred-fifty.

During the calm days, I used the Thrane & Thrane to post some gorgeous pictures of the Indian Ocean on my blog.

Then, just like that, the weather changed again.

On May 30, I had twenty knots of wind and was racing along in sunny days and starry nights. By the next morning, I had twenty-five to thirty knots and some pretty big seas. And by the night of June 1, the wind was at thirty-five knots gusting to forty-five, with gnarly squalls and twenty-five-foot seas.

I had a lot of sail up—the full genoa (the big sail on the front of the boat)—and a triple-reefed main. *Wild Eyes* was heeled over pretty far, but the squalls had passed and the wind was steady, so I finished squaring the boat away and went to bed.

I hadn't been asleep long when another squall swept through. The pilot flipped into standby, the boat jibed, and I jumped out of bed. But just as I reached the companionway door, I heard the sound of rushing water.

Not water rushing along the hull, but water rushing *into the boat*.

The ocean was pouring into the back compartment and I had no idea where it was coming from. Grabbing my flashlight, I dove back there and was immediately drenched in icy water. I climbed back to the source of the main stream and saw that it was pouring in through the cockpit throttle mounting. The mounting had plunged underwater because of the jibe. Working quickly, I shut off the hatches to the rear compartment and went topside to get *Wild Eyes* under control.

Outside, rain poured from the sky not in drops but in streams so cold they felt polar. I had my harness on but hadn't bothered to put on my foul-weather gear—I didn't have time to. *Wild Eyes* was nearly flat on her side and the running backstay was stuck on the wrong side of the boom.

I clipped onto the boom and climbed out to its end. I would rather not have done that, but I had no other choice. I had to free the boom, so I held on out there as big swells rolled the boat all over the place. Between swells, I grabbed the backstay, worked it loose, then jumped off the boom to the relative safety of a heeled-over deck in a wicked squall.

Once I got the boat sorted out and back on track, I went below to survey the water damage. There was quite a bit of water in the back compartment, and I was in a hurry to get it all out before it reached my electronics. I flipped on the bilge pump, and helped it along by bailing with a bucket.

The bad news was my diesel heater was drenched. The fat leak had been spraying almost directly on it. Soaked to the skin, I changed into some dry clothes, but I was really beginning to feel the cold and couldn't stop shivering. I thought about going back to bed, but the sun was just coming up so I went back topside to get a look at the seas.

The swells were amazing! As big as three-story apartment buildings! Instead of going back to bed, I started surfing down these huge walls of water at thrilling speeds. The rides seemed to last forever!

That alone just about made up for the trouble during the night. Later, when I was talking with my mom, she told me I had done two hundred thirty-seven miles in one day. That was close enough to two-fifty for me. After hearing that, my day went from ranking pretty low to one of the best times of my trip.

 The next few days were a mixed bag of wet and dry, but by June 9, I'd been caught in a train of rough weather that lasted several days. Commanders' had forecast a very rough nine to twelve-hour period, including a trough, or depression, followed by a cold front with strong winds from the northwest. The winds would be sustained from thirty-five to fifty knots, with gusts to sixty.

This was not good news. The string of rough weather had beaten *Wild Eyes* up pretty badly. One day a vicious wind tore my genoa. Another day the sail ties on my mainsail came loose and forty-five knot winds flogged it all over the place as I tried to tie it down again. The sail repairs were crucial, but I began to get behind on the rest of my workload. Then on June 10, the most furious storm in the series knocked *Wild Eyes* down four times.

That was the day I tried to start my engine to charge my batteries, but heard only a "click." I had to call home to make sure I got it right the first time. My batteries were too low to risk getting it wrong. Mom, Jeff, Dad, and Scott got on the bridge, but the satellite must have been busy elsewhere because the call kept dropping. In between drops, though, my dad told me to flip the compression lock lever. That would hold the exhaust valves open and enable the engine to turn over, and pump out the seawater. I followed Dad's instructions and got the engine running.

Between the wind and the machine-shop rattle of the engine, I couldn't hear what my parents and Jeff were saying. I yelled into the phone: *"Okay, I need to get some more water out of the boat! I'll call you back when I'm done!"*

I waited a second for an answer, but nobody said anything so I figured the call had dropped again. I put the phone back on the charger in my chart desk, clasped the desk lid shut, and got moving.

Outside, the wind had really picked up again. The roar turned into a high-pitched scream. I let the engine run for a while, keeping an eye on my battery power, then shut it down.

Setting the cover back on the engine box, I began flipping the latches shut. I had nearly flipped the third one closed when an invisible hand picked me up and flung me across the cabin.

My back slammed into the bulkhead above my bed, and my head hit the hard metal gauges. My vision went fuzzy. A howling roar filled the cabin like a jet engine, and the boat heeled crazily to port.

Now I was *lying* on the bulkhead . . . and not popping back up again. This wasn't a knockdown.

I'm rolling, I thought blearily, and the world went black.

CHAPTER 15
NIGHTMARE AT SEA

40.513 SOUTH/74.457 EAST
JUNE 2010

Seconds later, I woke up lying on the roof with things falling on top of me. The engine box cover, the teakettle, my toolbag, loose tools that I had just been using—all hitting me in the chest, legs, face. The sea had turned *Wild Eyes* upside down.

It was dark. Something had fallen on top of the cabin light, turning the cabin into a black tunnel. I couldn't hear anything at all. The roll didn't stop. It continued to port, and for just a few seconds I was sitting on the ceiling in the dark.

My head felt groggy but my thoughts tried to swim through it. *I'm on the roof. I'm upside down. Is this real?*

I was in complete disbelief. To make myself believe it, I said out loud to the darkness, "I'm rolling."

It was real. I had heard myself say so.

Then I was crashing down the starboard bulkhead, my body tearing through the galley. I tried to slow myself, grabbing at the stove, the handles—anything—but it didn't help. And then I was sitting on the cabin floor, a foot of water sloshing around me.

The roll stopped. *Wild Eyes* was upright.

Whatever had fallen on the cabin light had fallen some more, unblocking it. I could see again. Worse, I could think again. Even without looking I knew: *There is no way I still have a mast.*

Without a mast, the trip was over. Everything we had worked for, all the fund-raising, the training, all the prep, the jury-rigging, the brutal days at sea, gone in a couple of seconds.

Head still swimming, I stood in the flooded cabin and rummaged around until I came up with a flashlight. I could feel my heart beating in my throat. Fear rose in me like a stamping racehorse, but I refused to let it out of the gate.

Keep calm! I told myself. *Act.*

I tried to open the companionway door, but a tangle of lines blocked it partway shut. The mast had fallen and pulled the lines tight across the door. I had to go back inside and get a knife and slice through them to get up into the cockpit.

Outside, the temperature had plunged and the icy wind nearly knocked me over, stinging my face with sea spray. That cleared my head a little. The moon had turned bright and my eyes went straight to the deck where the mast should have been. The only thing left was a one-inch stub. Fifty feet of mast lay in the heaving water, downed lines and shrouds holding it there. The mast's sheared-off end poked up onto the deck. My broken boom was lying across the cockpit, useless as a bent nail.

My heart sank. I had been hoping that something of the mast had survived, and that the boom was still whole. Anything straight and tall that I could somehow lash together, jury-rig a sail, and push on to Kerguelen Island, a little rock I'd seen on my charts, or maybe even Australia. Save the boat and myself even if it took a month.

Sailors are great jury-riggers. Robin Lee Graham was dismasted twice during his solo journey. I remembered seeing a picture of him making way under the power of a sail he'd rigged up from a bed sheet patched up with bits of a hand towel and a T-shirt. Sails weren't my problem, though. I had spares below. But I had nothing aboard I could use for a mast.

Wild Eyes rocked wildly, drifting up one side of the swells and down the other under the dark bowl of the night. The screaming wind stung my face with salt, and a feeling I'd never had before washed over me: helplessness. I pictured *Wild Eyes* from the sky, my mind's eye pulling back, pulling back, higher and wider as if I were seeing her from an aerial camera. In the dead center of the Indian Ocean, my boat would look like a tiny white speck, like any other breaking wave.

Fear rose up in my chest again. I knew that even if I was able to call for help, I was in a place so remote that it wasn't likely there would be anyone who could help me. And even if there were, it could take weeks.

As *Wild Eyes* rolled in the heavy seas, I saw the way the mast was attached, keeled over into the water, its broken end poking up like a giant fractured bone. The mast wasn't in a position where it might damage the hull. For now it would keep the boat stable, like a sea anchor. Meanwhile, the dizziness was creeping back into my head again and I knew if I tried to cut the fallen mast away now, I'd put myself in unnecessary danger.

In that moment, a battle began in my mind. One part of my brain yelled at me: *Do something! Figure this out! Save your trip!*

The other part knew: *There's nothing you can do. It's over.*

I decided it was time to go let somebody know.

Going below, I shut the hatch against the wreckage outside and handed my way across the flooded cabin toward the chart desk and my Iridium phone. Even though my head felt swimmy, I did remember putting one phone back on the charger so that it could reconnect to the satellites before I called the team back about my engine.

But when I got to the desk, I saw for the first time that the clasp holding my chart desk closed had come undone. The lid had fallen open and both my phones were gone.

Kneeling on the chart desk seat, I pointed the flashlight down at the water sloshing in the cabin floor. It looked like the aftermath of a mini-hurricane. Charts, pencils, pens, batteries floating everywhere. My kitten calendar floated past, a drenched little tabby looking up at me pathetically. I plunged my arm down in the water up to my elbow, felt around for a moment until I felt a phone. I fished it out. It was as dead as a block of wood, water streaming out from around the buttons.

Not good.

As I sat all the way up, my head spun. Aiming the flashlight around the cabin, I realized everything was soaked. The seriousness of my situation started to sink in, and again I fought panic. I pushed it down, but it was harder this time, like my insides were an open can of shaken soda, and I was trying to keep it from bubbling up out of the top.

Not being able to make way in my boat was one thing. Not being able to communicate was something else. I knew one thing: I had to find my back-up phone, and it had to work. It *had* to. I stood and handed my way around the cabin, walking on the edge of the lidless engine box, the edge of my fold-up bed, jabbing the flashlight beam into every dark corner.

There!

A green light caught my eye. The phone! Somehow, it had flown from the chart desk and wedged itself between the alternator belt and the inside of the engine box wall, below the water hoses!

My heart soared and I almost shouted with relief.

Maybe it didn't get wet. Maybe it works!

I bent over the engine box and carefully pulled the phone from its miraculous little nook. The screen was lit up green, but it was blank and frozen. I pushed a couple of buttons, but nothing happened. I shook it. Still frozen. More buttons. Nothing. Finally, I decided to try recycling the power. I whispered a prayer, pushed the power button, and watched the screen go dark. I pushed Power again. But the screen stayed dark. The phone was dead.

In that moment it dawned on me that everything has to line up perfectly for something to turn out this awful. I sat down on the step leading out to the cockpit and glanced up.

"Lord," I said out loud, "how long were you planning this?"

Sitting on the step, I knew I had only one option left. I had to set off my EPIRBs, my emergency beacons. But that irrational battle started raging in my brain again. I had been through so much with my boat. I knew her forward and backward. I had fixed so many breakdowns, survived so many things.

I knew I was in the dead center of the Indian Ocean. Still I wondered, irrationally for the circumstances, *How long could I last out here? Weeks? Even months?*

Hope whispered in my head: *Maybe I could drift to Australia . . .*

Then the voice of reason stomped down: *Yeah, or be smashed on some rocks or run over by a large ship.*

Still . . .

You're fine, Hope said. *You've got plenty of food and you can make water.*

Reason: *Or you could roll again. Or another wave could slam the mast into the hull. Or a really big one could tear off your keel, then the boat wouldn't right herself.*

Get a grip!

Not even moving my head, I slid my eyes up and to the left. The EPIRB hung from a bracket on the wall just over my bed. Slowly, I turned my chin and stared at the device. Setting off the EPIRB would be making it official.

It would be Ending My Trip.

Admitting Defeat.

Setting it off meant I was giving up. That's something I don't do, or even consider. If you consider giving up, I had always reasoned, it becomes a possibility.

I felt the little fingers of magical thinking trying to tickle my mind again . . . *if you don't set it off, the trip's not over . . .*

I cut the thought off cold, stood, walked from the step to the edge of the engine box, leaned over, and took the EPIRB off the wall. Returning to the step, I sat again and held the white box in my hand. A little flap covered the manual activation switch and the box itself was plastered with all these warning stickers about not setting the thing off unless you were in grave danger. I felt so wrong about setting it off. I knew I could last for weeks out here and somehow, I felt like I should try.

Floodwater slapped against the step, the wind screamed outside, and I sat still as a rock, fighting both sides in a mental war. The determined sailor in me knew, *knew* that if I just waited a couple of days, some solution would materialize and I could save myself. But the rational part of me knew that was all wishful thinking. I'd eventually have to activate the EPIRB and the longer I waited, the more trouble I could be in. Besides, if even a day went by and no one at home heard from me, they'd all worry something terrible had happened. Which it had.

I slid the flap aside.

They're going to be able to see where I am, but I'm so far out, there's not going to be anything they can do about it, I thought. *That's just going to make it that much worse for my parents.*

I flipped the switch and a bright, white light began to pulse in my face. Flipping that switch was the hardest thing I ever had to do.

 "She'll call back," Marianne said when Abby fell off the bridge during the call about repairing her engine.

"We're up, we might as well stay up," Laurence said. "I'll go put on the coffee."

Ten minutes later, the Sunderlands sat in front of Marianne's computer with steaming mugs of Trader Joe's coffee. Jeff and Scott were still on the bridge discussing Abby's general state of mind.

"She sounded a lot better after she got it started," Scott said.

"Yeah, she was pretty frustrated when she first called," Jeff said. "Especially when the call kept dropping. How long before she hits the next storm?"

With a couple of keystrokes, Marianne pulled up the latest report from Commanders' Weather. Sipping his coffee, Laurence read it aloud over her shoulder. "Looks like she'll have strong winds from the northwest. Thirty-five to fifty knots, squalls to sixty."

"If she actually gets into that, she may have to heave to and ride it out," Scott said.

The four continued game planning for Abby's next battle with nature, while waiting for her to call back. Thirty-five minutes had passed when Laurence's cell phone rang from his nightstand.

"There she is," Laurence said. Carrying his coffee, he walked the few steps into the bedroom, wondering why Abby hadn't called back on Jeff's line. But when he picked up the phone in the dark bedroom, the screen showed an unfamiliar number.

"Who the devil is calling me at 4:45 in the morning?" he wondered aloud.

Laurence walked back to lean in the office doorway, punched the talk button, put the phone to his ear, and grinned at his wife. "G'day, this is Laurence Sunderland speaking. How may I help you at quarter to five in the morning?"

"Mr. Sunderland, this is the Coast Guard Center in Alameda, California. We've just had an activation of an emergency beacon."

Laurence put his hand over the phone and said to Marianne, "It's the Coast Guard. They've received a signal from Abby's EPIRB."

His mind flashed to Jessica Watson, the Australian teen sailor who was four months ahead of Abby's sail. She'd had a beacon go off after a knockdown.

Laurence put the call on speaker so that Marianne could hear. "Yes, I'm sure that's my daughter's boat. She's had several knockdowns earlier today. One of them probably set off her water-activated EPIRB."

"Well, sir, we can't tell whether the beacon was water activated, but we do believe it was intentionally activated."

Marianne's eyes went on alert. Laurence sat down next to her, holding the phone.

"But we've just spoken with Abigail not thirty minutes ago, and she was fine," Laurence said. "Could it be a delayed signal?"

What he was asking was, since she'd been knocked down earlier and was so far away, was it possible that the beacon had been activated then but the signal had only just been received by Alameda?

"No," the Coast Guard officer said. "The beacon was set off ten minutes ago and we received the signal eight minutes ago."

Laurence's confidence slipped a notch, but he kept his voice light. "Well, as I said, we've just spoken with Abigail and she's been through the worst of it. The storm was dying down. Let's check the beacon registration numbers and see which one it is."

Without a word, Marianne rose to dig the EPIRB folder from the file cabinet near her desk. Laurence snatched a pen off Marianne's desk and began scribbling the long series of numbers that came over the speakerphone: 2DD428063F81FE0.

Marianne laid the folder on the desk and opened it. Since Abby had three emergency beacons registered with the National Oceanic and Atmospheric Administration, the folder contained three nearly identical papers titled "Official 406 MHz Registration Form." Marianne quickly scanned the pages. Then her eyes landed on a check-marked box next to the words "Category II (Manual Deployment)."

The number next to the words seemed to leap off the page: 2DD428063F81FE0.

She pointed to the number and locked eyes with her husband. An exact match. Proof that Abby had intentionally activated her beacon.

Laurence willed his voice to remain calm. "What do we do from here? What region do we contact?" he asked the Coast Guard officer.

Crisp and efficient, the officer told Laurence that the American Coast Guard had already notified rescue authorities in Australia and La Reunion Island. Then he gave Laurence the contact information for both.

"Thanks very much," Laurence said. "We've got work to do."

He flipped back to the other line, where Scott and Jeff were still chatting on the bridge. "Sorry I've got to butt in here, guys, but Abigail has set off her EPIRB. We've got a search-and-rescue situation."

"Do you want me to come over?" Jeff asked immediately. "I can get showered and dressed and come over."

"It's going to be a crazy day," Laurence ventured.

"I'm coming over," Jeff said.

"Alright, we'll see you here," Laurence said. "I'm calling Reunion Island."

 I didn't know whether rescuers would be able to tell for sure that I'd set off the EPIRB by hand, or whether it had been water activated, so I found my MicroPLB (Personal Locator Beacon), and activated that, too. The PLB is the kind of beacon that pilots attach to their flight suits. An EPIRB might tell you where a vessel is, but the PLB will tell you where the person is. When I pulled the pin on that one, I knew my message would be underlined: *The EPIRB didn't go off by accident; I really need help.*

I had retrieved the PLB from my ditch bag, which was stored in an aft compartment. Now, walking forward again, I noticed that I was moving very slowly. I had a lot on my mind and it felt like an actual physical load on my shoulders, weighing me down. The worst part was that I knew how worried everyone would be. They might even think

I was dead, though I hoped the fact that I set off the PLB would help with that. The great thing about *Wild Eyes*—and one of the reasons my dad and I chose her—was that as long as I was inside her, I would be safe. I might be uncomfortable, maybe even miserable, but I would be okay. With all the food I had, I could've sailed around the world three times.

As I picked my way through the flooded cabin, I thought about the EPIRB again. When I pushed that button, I felt like I was proving the critics right. I knew it could've happened to anybody. It *had* happened to even the greatest sailors, like Isabelle Autissier, who was rolled in the very same ocean. Strangely, I hated it that I'd have to chalk up the accident to "bad luck" or "fate" or "providence" or whatever term you want to use when something bad happens and it's out of your control. It was weird, but I almost wished there was something I could blame my failure on, something I could've done differently. Instead, I felt completely helpless, and at that moment, that was even worse.

I reached underneath the chart desk to flip on the bilge pumps. I didn't know how long I would be adrift and it was important to start getting *Wild Eyes* in as good order as possible to prevent deterioration. I found my bucket and did some bailing, heaving pails half full of seawater out the companionway door and into the cockpit. The sky was still dark and stormy. Cold winds whistled down into the cabin. By the time I had pitched the third bucket of water, my head reeled and I had to sit down on the step.

The inside of the cabin looked soft to me—the edges of the chart desk, the engine box, my bed—all fuzzy like a worn blanket. My face felt flushed. I bent forward and put my head on my knees. Then I saw water from my hair dripping onto my feet, and noticed for the first time how really wet I was. My clothes were soaked through from my neck to my toes. After the roll, did I even have any more dry clothes? I wasn't sure. Suddenly, I was very, very cold.

Shivering, I stood up. Gripping the bulkhead handholds, I crept unsteadily toward the bow and forward sail compartment. It seemed so far away. I moved slowly, *Wild Eyes* rocking beneath me. Right then, the thought of falling into any kind of water again seemed unbearable. Suddenly, I wanted to be warm and dry more than I had wanted anything, ever. As I reached the sail compartment door, I sent up a silent prayer: *Lord, please let it be dry in there.*

Twisting the latch on the Plexiglas door, I opened it and there it was, a little refuge. The only dry spot for seven hundred miles in one direction and two thousand miles in all others. The compartment was piled high with food stores, clothes in bags, neglected schoolbooks, and computer accessories. My big Code Zero sail covered the top of everything. I leaned in and rummaged around until I found a pair of blue Capilene base layer pants, and a couple of long-sleeved shirts. I shucked my wet clothes inside the cabin, then crawled up on top of the sails to put on the dry ones.

I was still really dizzy, though. Reaching back, I felt the back of my head where it had crashed into the B&G gauges. There was a knot the size of half a walnut and it was tender. Did I have a concussion? I knew that if you had a concussion, you weren't supposed to go to sleep. Maybe some fresh air would clear my head.

Handing my way carefully back to the companionway, I stayed on top of everything, not wanting to get my dry clothes wet again. Outside, though, the waves were rough and *Wild Eyes* was rolling gunwale to gunwale. A wave crashed over the boat, sending a rain of mist down my front, and I ducked back into the cabin to keep from getting any wetter.

Then, exhaustion hit me like a rogue wave all its own. It was all I could do to get back to the sail locker, crawl up on the Code Zero, and close the Plexiglas door behind me. To conserve power, I left all the lights off, but the EPIRB light pulsed eerily, light and dark, light and dark.

Suddenly, I felt the hugeness of my isolation. I thought of Kerguelen Island, the tiny rock I had seen on my charts. As far as I knew, the only people who lived there were penguins. At this point, I thought they'd be pretty good company.

The sail compartment was small and cramped and I had to hunch over and root around to find my spare sleeping bags. I had brought two extra ones, along with a spare pillow, in waterproof bags and now I was thankful for them. Piled on top of the Code Zero, the bags and pillow made a pretty nice bed under the circumstances. But every time I closed my eyes, I felt like I was rolling, rolling, falling down *Wild Eyes'* walls again. It was the worst feeling I'd ever felt.

It was like a horrible movie clip, only worse, because I could *feel* it—not just see it. The boat rolling . . . not popping up . . . just rolling 360 degrees in slow motion. In the dark compartment, I opened my eyes wide.

Think about something else . . . what's going to happen next? What do I need to clean up on the boat tomorrow?

. . . but as soon as my eyes slipped closed again, I was falling and falling and falling. I didn't want to keep replaying it, but I couldn't make it go away. This was a strange and terrible feeling for me because I'm usually not the type to wallow in the past. My way is to deal with things and move on. So besides the fact that these flashbacks were bothering me, I was bothered that they were bothering me! Gradually, though, a new concern edged that one out: *pain*.

I hadn't realized how numb I was from the cold. After huddling down in the sleeping bags for about fifteen minutes, I began to warm up and when I did, I really started to hurt. My leg, where the engine box cover had fallen on it, felt swollen and bruised. My head, where I hit the gauge, still throbbed. My whole back ached. But it was my right foot that screamed the loudest.

I could live with the rest of it, but my foot yelled, "Pay attention to me!" Pulling my legs out of the sleeping bag, I shined the flashlight on them and saw that my foot was covered in a sheet of sticky crimson. I hadn't been able to feel it before, but now I could see a deep gash about an inch long oozing fresh blood.

Scrunched up in the tiny space, I rooted around for my medical kit. But it was a halfhearted search. My arms and legs felt like lead and the more I moved around, the more I hurt. Finally I found a T-shirt and wrapped it tightly around my foot to keep pressure on it. Exhausted, I lay back down and resigned myself to falling and falling. And sometime during the night, I finally fell asleep.

When a ringing telephone awakened Michael Wear, he rolled over and glanced at the clock. It was 2:00 a.m. Usually not a good sign.

He picked up his mobile. "Michael Wear speaking."

The caller was John Fornell, Wear's colleague from the Water Police branch of the Western Australian Police Force (WAPF). Wear listened carefully as Fornell explained that the young American girl who had been sailing solo around the world had activated two of her emergency beacons.

Wear worked as search-and-rescue coordinator for the WAPF. "Where is the signal coming from?" he asked.

"From the center of the Indian Ocean."

It was a bit of a shock. "That's a long way out," Wear said.

In fact, if you could pick a spot on earth to be farthest from land, that would be it. But the beacon location was just inside Australia's search-and-rescue jurisdiction. Australian Maritime Safety in Canberra had received the initial notification of the distress call and was asking for Western Water Police assistance, along with staff volunteers to man a rescue flight.

"Canberra has chartered a Qantas Airbus for use as a search plane," Fornell said. "We're all heading out to Perth International."

By now Wear's wife, Karen, had awakened and was listening to the end of her husband's conversation. When he hung up, he filled her in.

"Well, I'm down to South Africa."

"What? When?"

"Now."

Wear explained that Abigail Sunderland, the American girl who was sailing solo around the world, had sent out distress signals. "She's about two thousand miles to the southwest, between here and South Africa. I've been asked to get my passport and head to the airport. We're going to fly out and try to locate her."

Wear had little time, but little need to take much with him. All he took from home was a daypack with his passport (in case the Qantas jet had to land in another country), and the Australia search-and-rescue manual.

At the airport in Perth, he met up with a colleague, Peter Trivett, a senior constable with the Water Police, and a dozen volunteers from State Emergency Services (SES), who would act as "spotters." The only additional equipment Trivett had brought was a direction finder and a small portable VHF marine radio. The Qantas jet would have the sophisticated equipment necessary to locate Abby's satellite beacon signal. But Wear and his colleagues suspected that verbal communications with the girl would require something a bit lower tech: a handheld marine band radio.

At the airport in Perth, Wear briefed the Qantas crew. A French fishing vessel, *Ile de la Reunion*, had been plying the waters around Kerguelen Island. Its captain, Paul-Louis LeMoigne, had agreed to volunteer his ship as the rescue platform, and he had already diverted his vessel toward satellite coordinates provided by Canberra. But *La Reunion* was at least four hundred miles from *Wild Eyes'* last known position and it would take LeMoigne at least thirty hours to reach her.

Wear, Trivett, the Qantas crew, and the SES spotters boarded the Airbus, buttoned up, and taxied to the runway. Perth tower issued clearance and the Qantas jet took off into the dark night, bound for one of the most remote places on earth, to help save the life of a young girl no one on board had ever met.

Reunion Island rises from the Indian Ocean east of Madagascar. Found uninhabited by Portuguese sailors in 1635, the island has been in French possession since 1642 when Jacques Pronis of France deported a dozen French mutineers there. Reunion is now home to an ethnic mix of European, African, Malagasy, Indian, and Chinese origin. But when Laurence Sunderland, his gut twisted with worry, called the island to check the status of search-and-rescue efforts for his daughter, the man who answered the phone spoke mostly French.

Laurence was able to discern that *oui*, they'd received a beacon signal, and that *oui*, *les Américains* had called on the *téléphone* about a boat in *difficulté*. But when the man went on to speak rapidly about *recherché et de sauvetage*, Laurence knew the language barrier was wasting precious minutes. As politely as he could, he asked if he could *téléphone* back in a few *moments*. Then he hung up and bolted for the bedroom door.

"I'll be right back," he called to Marianne. "I'm going to get Marianne Preston."

This Marianne was the wife of Rick Preston, and their daughters were good friends with the Sunderland girls. The family lived up the street and Marianne was a high school French teacher. With Laurence gone, Marianne Sunderland decided the first thing she would do was get as many people as she could praying on behalf of their daughter. Her heart pounding, she tapped out e-mails to Christian friends as far away as Russia, asking them to pray for Abby's safe return. Then she sat back in her chair and let her mind work.

Who else can help? Who else can get the word out?

Marianne called Scott. They discussed issues that had arisen during Zac's trip and the capacities of smaller rescue operations. Neither Marianne nor Scott knew much about Reunion Island, except that it was a tiny tourist spot. And they knew nothing about the island's SAR capabilities.

An idea struck Marianne. "Do you think it would be a good idea to inform the media? That might raise public awareness of the situation."

"Yeah, I think it probably would," Scott said.

A name flashed into Marianne's mind: Marc Dorian.

Marc was an avid sailor who worked as a producer at ABC's *20/20*. The Sunderlands had gotten to know him at the beginning of Abby's trip when ABC did a segment on young record-setters called "How Young Is Too Young?"

Hunting up Marc's number on her cell phone, Marianne pushed SEND and was relieved when he answered. She explained what had happened and asked whether Marc thought it would be a good idea to put out a story. Maybe it would bring national or even international attention that would help.

Within two hours, a story with Marc Dorian's byline appeared on abcnews.com. And two hours after that, Calle Margarita, a sleepy little suburban street in Thousand Oaks, California, was jammed with reporters, satellite trucks, and cameras.

 On the marathon flight to the middle of nowhere, rescue spotters on the Qantas plane napped, read, and chatted quietly. Michael Wear passed the time by reviewing some parts of the Australian search-and-rescue manual he hadn't had the occasion to touch on in his brief career in search and rescue—specifically the procedures in relation to vessels in distress in another country's jurisdiction.

The Canberra rescue center had provided the Qantas flight crew with a satellite-generated waypoint—coordinates to fly toward—in the approximate middle of twenty-seven million square miles of ocean. As the flight entered its sixth hour, the cockpit crew nosed the jet into a gradual descent from forty thousand feet. Wear felt a tingle of anticipation, of hope surging against long odds. He sensed the atmosphere change in the rest of the cabin too. Casual conversations stopped, seat backs came forward, and the rescue spotters began peering out the cabin windows.

The Qantas pilot told the spotters he was descending to fifteen hundred feet in order to try and spot *Wild Eyes*. Wear didn't know quite what to expect at that altitude: what the weather would be; what visibility would be like through the aircraft windows; and whether— if someone could spot Abby's boat—it would be upright or capsized. Wear had briefed the Qantas cockpit crew for either contingency.

If the vessel was upright, the pilot was to descend as low as he could and make as much noise as possible in order to alert Abby to their presence.

Wear's team was also aware that *Wild Eyes* was equipped with a rear escape hatch, so if they found the boat capsized, the plan was much different. In that case, the Airbus would keep its distance because the rescue team did not want Abby to hear the plane and come out of the escape hatch. Since the fishing-boat-turned-rescue-vessel, *La Reunion*, was still at least twenty-four hours away, Wear's team didn't want to risk the possibility of water rushing in through the escape hatch.

When the Qantas jet reached fifteen hundred feet, Wear and the other spotters could see heavy seas below. White caps slid across the dark gray sea like a ghostly fleet. Wear could tell the water was rough because of the length of time the white caps rolled down the faces of the waves. The sheer number of white caps concerned him. The chances of spotting *Wild Eyes* among them seemed slim.

 When the Sunderlands first understood that Abby had intentionally set off her EPIRBs, Marianne, the optimist, let her mind reel through all the possible positive outcomes. She remembers that it was almost as if her brain were shielding her heart, not allowing her to think of any worst-case scenario.

Always the realist, Laurence dealt with the situation differently. The satellites showed *Wild Eyes* drifting at a very slow rate. Therefore, *Wild Eyes* must have capsized, he concluded—the worst possible scenario, short of Abby already having drowned. If she had capsized while tied in on deck, his daughter had likely perished. If she had been below, the boat was still probably afloat, but Abby would be in complete darkness, without any way to communicate with the outside world. Also, if she was upside down in the water, the boat would probably be leaking badly, and Abby would have no way to bail out water. The only opening she would have access to was the escape hatch on the transom. And if she exited through it, she would be exposed to the icy Indian Ocean and could freeze to death before help came. If help could find her.

Marianne knew Abby's strength of spirit, and had grown to admire her daughter even more as she overcame challenge after challenge during her sail. But the thought of her daughter living through that kind of hell caused Marianne to tremble all over and weep in anguish over her sweet brave daughter who would no doubt be doing everything she could to stay alive.

Marianne tried to keep busy, sending out prayer requests, talking to family and friends. The Sunderlands' pastor and his wife came over to offer comfort and prayer. Jeff and Bill had arrived and were rocks of emotional support. They also helped answer the telephone and handle the press.

Marianne tried to stay hopeful. But slowly her imagination bull-dozed her optimism aside and pushed her mind into a dark place. There she saw Abby tethered to the boat in her bright red foul-weather gear, being dragged along dead in the sea.

 Morning came and I cracked my eyes, slowly remembering that I'd gone to sleep in the middle of a real live disaster movie. I tried to sit up, but overnight the pain in my body had hardened into stiffness and I could hardly move. Lying on top of the Code Zero, I decided to take it slowly, working my arms around a little, then my legs, wincing when the gash in my foot brushed against the sleeping bag zipper. Slowly, carefully, I climbed down out of the sail locker and into the cabin.

At first, my heart sank. The cabin looked exactly what you would expect a room to look like if it had been turned completely upside down, then right side up again. For a moment I sat down at the chart table. I knew I needed to get my bearings. I knew I needed to make a plan.

Sitting there, I remembered that while planning my trip, I had looked at my charts and noted a couple of places in the ocean so remote that it would be pretty much impossible to be rescued. The rogue wave had picked one of them in which to roll my boat. Australia, the nearest country with a rescue service of significant size, was more than two thousand miles away. Even if they sent a boat, it could take two weeks to reach me.

How long can I last out here? I wondered again. A rescue could take weeks, or if something went wrong with the beacons, even months.

I'll be out here as long as I need to be. That, as they say on TV, was my final answer.

I began preparing a mental list of the work I needed to do: Get the water-maker running. Get the engine running. Get the deck squared away. Keep brainstorming a way to rig up a mast.

Then I got moving.

Going topside, I picked my way carefully across the deck, lifting each foot high to avoid tripping on snarled lines. The sky was gray, but it looked to me like the sun might burn through. The seas were still big and breaking over the boat. Reaching the broken end of the mast, I peered over the side. All around me the sea was a foaming gray. But far below the surface where the mast entered the water, I saw the triangle of my staysail. The sight creeped me out. The sea heaved and fell, but weighted down by the water, the sail was as still as a corpse.

In Thousand Oaks, the Sunderlands had been up since Abby's first call at 4:00 a.m. Eight months pregnant and emotionally exhausted, Marianne couldn't bear the strain any longer and went to bed. While she slept, neighbors came over and fed and bathed the Sunderlands' little ones. Meanwhile, Zac and Jeff went outside occasionally to deal with the press.

Later that evening, when Marianne woke up, all the kids were in bed except Zac. She saw that some more friends had come over. The lights were dim and the house hushed with whispered prayers, low conversations, and quiet tears. Marianne sat down with her good friend Kristi Nash.

Meanwhile, Laurence had become quite worn down. The Sunderlands had been notified about the Qantas rescue flight and knew approximately when they'd hear news from the flyover. As the clock ticked toward that time, he slipped over the edge of emotional exhaustion. People came over to try and encourage him, but he only became more and more disheartened. Laurence was a *doer*, not someone who did well waiting to see what could be done.

If Abby wasn't okay, Marianne wondered whether he would survive it.

 Without my rig, it was hard to tell how fast the wind was blowing, but it was definitely up there, probably twenty-five to thirty knots. The seas were still steep. Before stepping out, I had put my harness on; then I climbed the steps topside and tied my harness to a pad eye mounted in the cockpit. Both handrails were broken, and all of the stanchions, too. Also, both of my lifelines were gone. Surveying my wrecked boat, I noticed some new damage that had happened in the night.

The lines had snapped on the boom and it had fallen into the water, punching a hole in the ballast tank. That wasn't a bad thing. *Wild Eyes* had two ballast tanks, one on each side of the boat. They could be filled with seawater, providing more stability.

Meanwhile, the mast's current position wasn't going to put the boat in danger. But if it shifted more it could puncture the hull below the water ballast tank. I decided to cut it loose.

I went below to try to find my hacksaw to cut through the rigging. After the roll, who knew where it would be? But this time, I caught a break. The saw had landed conveniently next to my chart desk.

At that moment, all at once, a mental picture hit me: the vastness of the ocean spreading out around me, my boat no bigger than an especially large fish. I took a sip of water and panic rose in my chest. The only thing I knew to do was to pray.

"Lord, if I'm going to be rescued," I said out loud, "please let me know."

Even as I said it, I knew it was a ridiculous thing to pray. I mean, I was out in the middle of the Indian Ocean, one of the remotest places on earth. What was God going to do, send a carrier pigeon?

Shaking my head at myself, I decided to go topside again. I tied in and put the blade to work on some lines at the back of the boat. The icy cold was actually a good thing. It cleared my head and numbed the pain of my injuries, which meant I could work to get the boat in shape for what might be a very long wait.

Suddenly a big swell rocked *Wild Eyes*. My heart jumped into my throat. I grabbed the steel arch at the stern with a death grip. My heart raced and I glanced wildly around me.

But the seas looked normal. Choppy with big swells, but nothing to worry about. I felt my face flush. Even though there wasn't another living soul within hundreds of miles, I was embarrassed. And the feeling didn't go away. Against reason, I kept thinking that the next swell would be it: another rogue wave would roll me again, and I'd be stuck underwater tied to the top of the boat. It was so unlike me to be afraid this way. Hadn't I just sailed twelve thousand miles? Hadn't I been having a blast surfing the fronts of thirty-foot waves just twenty-four hours before? What had happened to me?

Shake it off! I told myself. *That's why they're called "rogue" waves, stupid. They don't happen very often.*

I knew worrying about it wouldn't help. "Get the rigging off," I said aloud. "That's what will make a difference."

At that moment, a noise from above caught my attention. And I looked up just in time to see a gigantic white airplane fly by.

 "Contact, left-hand side!" It was Michael Wood, a Qantas flight attendant who had volunteered for the mission. "I see her!"

A cheer went up in the cabin. Both the SES volunteers and the flight crew marked Abby's position on GPS, while Wear marveled at the accuracy of the EPIRBs and satellite system. When the Qantas crew spotted Abby, the Airbus was no more than three hundred meters away from her boat. The satellite had generated so accurate a fix that the Airbus had literally flown straight to *Wild Eyes'* position, a relative speck in the middle of the third-largest body of water on earth.

 When I saw that plane, I was absolutely astonished! I knew I hadn't hit my head *that* hard. There was a no-kidding, honest-to-God passenger jet in the middle of the Indian Ocean where *no one ever flies.* And this one was flying super low. They were definitely looking for me! There was nothing else they could have been doing way out here!

Two emotions crashed over me: surging joy and crazy fear. Instantly, the fear trampled over the joy like a herd of wild horses. That moment was the most frightened I had ever been. I knew if that plane didn't see me *right then*, they'd be gone, off to search somewhere else in the massive waters of the Indian Ocean. If that happened, I wasn't going to be getting home. Ever.

Already the plane was nearly past me and I couldn't tell if they had seen me.

I need to let them know I'm here! I'm here and I'm alive!

Racing below, I flew to the chart desk and flipped my radio on.

 The Qantas pilot put the Airbus in a banking turn and began to circle *Wild Eyes'* position. Pete Trivett keyed up the marine VHF radio and began trying to raise Abby.

"*Wild Eyes, Wild Eyes*, this is Qantas Rescue Flight, how do you hear me?"

The next moment was one Wear will never forget. He felt an incomparable shiver of relief and joy as he heard a young woman with an American accent say very calmly, "This is *Wild Eyes*."

 It's not every day that you see your prayers answered so powerfully and literally. When something good happens after people pray, sometimes they think, well that was going to happen anyway—it doesn't mean it was God who did it. But I had prayed, "Lord, if I'm going to be rescued, please let me know."

And then, minutes later, a giant plane flies over the exact spot where I am in an ocean that covers twenty-seven million square miles! *That* wasn't going to happen anyway!

The things that happen on the sea take you beyond yourself, beyond human capability. A lot of people go to sea lukewarm about God and come back fiery believers. It happened to my brother, and now it had happened to me.

In the cabin, I threw back my head and laughed out loud. "Thank you, God. Thank you!"

 Wear had a list of questions from the Rescue Coordination Center, questions that would be used to elicit vital information. But the range of the VHF radios was very short, which meant that flying over *Wild Eyes* at 250 knots allowed a window of just ten to fifteen seconds to exchange information with Abby. Taking over the handheld from Trivett during the aircraft's first pass, Wear asked, "Are you physically okay?"

"Yes, I am fine," Abby said.

On the Airbus's second pass, Wear could see that *Wild Eyes*' mast was down on the starboard side and that the sails were in the water. He asked if Abby's vessel was watertight.

"Yes, my boat is watertight," Abby replied. Wear noticed that the young American sounded very much in control. Like a woman who knew exactly what she was doing and what she had to do next in order to survive.

On the third pass, Abby let Wear know that her sat phone was down and the VHF radio was her only means of communication. And on the fourth, Wear tried to let Abby know that a rescue vessel was en route and would reach her in twenty-four hours.

But to that, there was no reply. Wear kept transmitting the information, trying to tell Abby that *La Reunion* was steaming toward her position. But still no answer. Wear speculated that Abby might have turned off her radio to conserve power.

The Airbus continued to circle the area until its fuel load demanded a return to Australia. The cabin buzzed with excitement as the rescue volunteers celebrated their success in finding Abby. But as the Qantas pilot began his ascent and pointed homeward, a hollow feeling invaded Michael Wear's gut. Then an uneasy quiet seemed to spread through the whole cabin. The team had located Abby, yes. But they also had been forced to leave her in rough seas with no mast and no control over her boat. Now, all that Wear and his team could do was wait and hope.

 Laurence's phone rang and Bill picked it up. He handed the phone to Laurence, whose face was pinched with a strange mixture of hope and dread. Then Marianne saw his face light up and tears fill his eyes. The whole room listened on edge as Laurence repeated in breathless bursts what he was hearing:

"Her boat is upright! . . .

"The rig is down! . . .

"And she's fine! Those were Abby's words! 'I'm fine!'"

The living room erupted in a burst of joy, laughter, and tears. Chills, elation, hugs upon hugs. Marianne, who thought she had cried herself dry, burst into tears. Just like that, a single phone call erased one possible, horrendous future—and replaced it with the bright certainty that God had answered the prayers of thousands and that their beloved Abby was coming home.

 I heard them say that a rescue boat would reach my position in twenty-four hours! I couldn't believe it . . . I didn't think there would be any boats this far south.

Those next twenty-four hours flew by. Looking back, that seems strange; you would think the time would crawl, but it didn't. After speaking with the team aboard the Qantas jet, I ran topside and watched for a long time until it was only a speck of white against the hard blue sky.

Then I thought about what I could salvage. What could I take home? My computer was drenched. My spare computers were in the back compartment, which was sealed off and taking on water. My cameras, which I had been shooting footage with the day before, were soaked. Everything was soaked. Everything.

I started looking for my boat papers and passport, which had been in a waterproof file folder. I guess it must not have been all that waterproof, though, because as I was pawing through my chart desk looking for the folder, my passport fell—plop!—right on the desk in front of me.

I was like, "Oh, *there* it is!" It had been stuck to the ceiling ever since the roll. It was a funny moment in an unfunny situation, as though my passport knew how important it was and had just been waiting to jump down and surprise me.

Along with my passport, I collected a couple of necklaces that were special to me, and laid out a dry suit and survival suit in case, for some reason, I had to get in the water when the rescue boat came. After that I got back to work, tackling a list of things I needed to do in case no boat ever came.

I made water. I fixed the heater. I took a crack at repairing the engine, but couldn't get it working. The wind and seas grew calmer, and the sun broke through the clouds. The sunlight and the possibility of rescue seemed to fuel my body. All of a sudden I wasn't sore anymore. Wielding the hacksaw like a reverse boat builder, I crawled all over the deck, cutting through the shrouds that held the fallen mast against *Wild Eyes*. Several times I had to untie my harness and tie back in at a different spot. After I got down to business, I was surprised at how easily the shrouds came free. It took me about half an hour to cut through all four of them.

While I was sawing away, I hadn't realized that the hard work was providing me with a kind of mental sanctuary. That little window of time was the first time I had been awake when I was too busy to be afraid. But now the job was done. I went below and now I had time to think again.

I didn't want to think about what the Aussies had said, that a boat was coming to get me. I didn't want to get excited. I didn't want to get my hopes up because strangely, when I did, that's when the fear crept in, like bugs crawling through my brain. If I hoped to be saved in a day, I feared I wouldn't be saved for weeks. A few times I let myself dwell on that possibility too long and fear tried to suck me down like quicksand.

Just twelve hours after returning from the twelve-hour Qantas flight, Michael Wear drove to the airport at Perth again. The Rescue Coordination Center at Canberra had chartered a second spotter flight, a Global Express jet. This time three police officers were among the volunteers, including one who spoke fluent French. The Canberra rescue coordinators who had arranged for *La Reunion* to head for *Wild Eyes'* location had learned that the ship's entire crew was of French nationality and, as far as Canberra could learn, no one aboard spoke English. The French-speaking Aussie officer had a dual advantage: his family was from Reunion Island, the fishing vessel's home port.

Knowing the outbound leg to Abby's location was another six-hour flight, Wear and his team were anxious to get underway. But there was a problem: a mechanical issue with the aircraft. As jet mechanics worked to isolate and repair the malfunction, Wear pictured Abby alone, floating on her little stick of a boat, and felt precious minutes ticking by.

As the hours flew by, each time fear tried to worm its way into my brain, I stomped on it: *No!*

Whatever it took, I would keep my mind focused on making

a life on *Wild Eyes* for however long I needed to. I did have hope. That was the difference. Rescuers knew I was out here and alive. That meant my family would know.

Twenty-four hours after the rescue plane flew over, I sat down on the chart desk and turned the radio back on. It was one of those things where I hoped that when I flipped the switch, I'd immediately hear someone in the middle of a scratchy transmission, calling for *Wild Eyes*.

Instead there was only silence.

An hour passed, then another. But they passed like seconds. I could almost imagine the minute hand sweeping around the clock like a second hand, racking up one hour, then two, then three, then more.

Fear snuck up and whispered in my ear: *Maybe no one is coming.*

 Two more hours passed before the second rescue flight took off from Perth. Then, more than five hours from the Australian coast, the Global Express jet neared the new coordinates provided by Canberra. Peering down from a thousand feet, Wear could discern that the sea conditions had improved slightly. But a dark cloud layer obscured visibility from the air, and as the jet circled the area where Abby was supposed to be, the spotters couldn't find her.

The pilot banked around the satellite waypoint in a long low race-track pattern, but even with nearly twenty people visually scouring the ocean surface, there was no sign of *Wild Eyes*.

A knot of worry formed in Wear's chest. *What had happened to Abby?*

The jet circled *Wild Eyes'* last known position for nearly thirty minutes. Then Wear and his team received a fresh set of satellite coordinates from Canberra. The new waypoint was between twenty and thirty miles away and it took the aircraft only about five minutes to reach it. During that short ride, Wear reflected that without satellite technology, they could have searched and searched until their fuel ran out, and Abby, though just a few miles away, might never have been found.

When the jet reached the new waypoint, Wear was dismayed when he saw that the spotters' view of the sea was blocked by billowy gray rafts of cumulonimbus clouds. Raindrops mottled the aircraft's windows, making it nearly impossible for spotters to see the water. But then, quite suddenly, the weather cleared in a way that seemed miraculous to Wear. He would later say that "it was like the hands of God sort of came down and cleared the clouds for us."

 As much as I tried to squash my worries, they floated up to the surface of my mind again. Maybe the fishing boat was having trouble pinpointing my exact location. Or maybe my beacon had stopped working. Eventually I hopped down from the chart table, and grabbed my flare gun. I knew you could see a flare from thirty miles around. If I fired one and the rescue vessel was anywhere close, the crew should be able to spot it.

 Fifteen to twenty minutes after arriving at Canberra's new waypoint, rescuers spotted *Wild Eyes*. Wear began trying to raise Abby on the VHF. "*Wild Eyes*, this is Global Express rescue flight, how do you hear me?"

But there was no answer.

Wear transmitted again and again without success.

"*Wild Eyes*, the rescue vessel is very close now. If you can hear me, activate a flare so that the vessel can see your position."

Peter Trivett began using a digital camera with a high-power zoom lens to take still shots of the disabled boat. By comparing the stills, Trivett and Wear could see that Abby, clad in red foul-weather gear, was indeed standing on deck. It was possible that she was receiving Wear's transmissions but was unable to transmit.

 With the flare gun in my hand, I scrambled topside, my mind threatening to gallop off into panic. And the moment I reached the deck, I looked up and saw the strangest thing ever: *another* huge plane! A different one!

Instead of being overjoyed, terror stabbed at my heart. I couldn't think of a reason in the world why another plane would be way out here, unless rescuers had lost track of my position.

From below, I heard the radio squawk to life. "*Wild Eyes*, this is Global Express Rescue. How do you hear me? *Wild Eyes*, this is Global Express Rescue, do you copy? Over."

I couldn't tell if this plane had seen me, but it seemed to be moving past my position. Aiming the flare gun high, I fired a red missile into the sky. But the projectile seemed to arc up behind the jet's path as it flew away from me.

 Michael Wear saw a flare speeding directly—a little too directly—at the jet. But its red flames passed well beneath the plane. That let Wear and the crew know Abby was okay. *Now, where was the fishing boat?* Wear wondered.

Suddenly, I realized that the plane's radio transmission hadn't said they could see me. I dashed below and snatched up the mike. "This is *Wild Eyes*, do you read me? This is *Wild Eyes!* Can you hear me?"

My heart pounded in my chest. Why in the world was another plane out here? Twenty-four hours had come and gone long ago. Where was the promised rescue boat?

From the Global Express cockpit, Wear scanned the ocean surface. Then he saw something he will never forget. As the jet approached *Wild Eyes* from a distance of about half a mile, he could see the French vessel, *La Reunion*, a few miles off. Wear noticed that the rescue flight, *Wild Eyes*, and the fishing vessel formed three points on a perfect line. At that moment, it struck him how providentially the whole rescue had fallen into place. Even the Global Express flight's two-hour delay seemed to him divine timing. Had the jet taken off on time, fuel constraints would've forced an earlier return to Perth, meaning that Wear and his team would not have been on site to see the operation through to the end.

Glancing over at the EPIRB, I could still see its white light pulsing. Were the satellites receiving its signal? Was my position going through? The light was flashing, but that didn't mean a signal was actually pinging out to the satellite. And it didn't mean a satellite was near enough to pick up its signal. So many other things had gone wrong . . . the autopilot, the engine, the phones, the broken mast . . . why shouldn't the EPIRB malfunction, too?

Unable to make voice contact with this second plane I felt my chances were fading fast. Dropping the radio mic, I sprinted up to the deck . . .

. . . and saw a huge ship bearing down on me!

I almost jumped out of my skin! I didn't know where it had come from because I had just been outside moments before. But it was *right there*, so close I thought we were going to trade paint.

I learned later that the fishing vessel did not see my boat, but they did see me setting off the flare. And the rescue plane helped guide the ship to my exact location.

The ship's hull was painted dark blue, with a narrow strip of dark orange around the top of the hull just below the railing. I could see the vessel's name, *La Reunion*, painted near the bow. At first the ship was just kind of circling, and I was wondering how in the world I was going to get from my little boat that was rolling all over the place to their huge boat that was also rolling all over the place. But then I saw some of the crew members lowering a dinghy over the side with two men aboard. They motored over and pulled alongside me.

I later found out that one of the men in the dinghy was *La Reunion's* captain, Paul-Louis LeMoigne. Neither man spoke a lot of English and I spoke zero French, so we didn't have a lot of conversation during the transaction. But I knew I was supposed to get in the dinghy, so I made hand motions that said, "Wait, I'll be right back." Then I went below to grab the things I'd gathered to take with me. I didn't even have shoes on, just a few thermal layers and my red foul-weather gear.

The men in the dinghy grabbed one of *Wild Eyes'* stanchions so that their boat would ride up and down the swells along with mine. I turned to lower myself feet first into their boat and when I got close the crew grabbed me and pulled me into the dinghy.

The seas were still rough and dark, with waves from ten to twelve feet. We motored over to *La Reunion*, where a rope ladder hung down. From high above, one of the crew members threw a line down into the dinghy and the men in the dinghy secured it to me in case I fell in. Just as I was about to grab the rope ladder, a huge swell lifted the dinghy nearly to *La Reunion's* deck level, and at least a dozen smiling French fishermen pulled me aboard.

As soon as Abby was safely aboard *La Reunion*, one of the crew members led her to the bridge, where Michael Wear was waiting on the other end of a satellite phone.

"This is Michael Wear of Australian search and rescue. How are you?

Abby first words were: "Has anyone called my parents?"

"As soon as you and I ring off, I'm going to call the Rescue Center in Canberra and have them call your parents. That's the first call I'm going to make—to make sure your parents know that you're okay."

Wear noticed that Abby sounded tired, worn down. Like someone who had been tough for as long as it took. Perhaps, he thought, she was coming to terms with the fact that her trip was over and she was leaving behind *Wild Eyes*, the sturdy little vessel that had saved her life.

The rescue flight circled above *La Reunion* as long as fuel would permit, then the pilot turned the jet toward Perth. Unlike the somber flight home the day before, this cabin buzzed with the thrill of success. Wear and his team were overjoyed, having just completed one of the most difficult and significant rescue operations Australia had ever been involved in—and in terms of the remote location, possibly one of the most significant marine rescue operations across the world.

"There was certainly an air of excitement and fulfillment that we completed the job, and the satisfaction of knowing that we're part of a worldwide system that works," Wear would later say. "For me, to be personally involved in an operation of such magnitude is probably one of the pinnacles of the field that I'm in."

From the bridge, I was able to call home. When I heard my mom's and dad's voices for the first time, a wave of relief flowed through me. I was just so happy to talk to my family—there were times while I waited for my rescue when I thought I might never see them again.

"Hi Abby! We are so glad you are okay!"

"Thanks, Mom."

"Are you hurt?"

"No. I hit my head when I rolled and that hurts, but otherwise I'm fine."

"Okay, if you feel anything weird, like dizzy or nauseous, you tell some-one right away. There could be internal injuries that you're unaware of."

"Okay, Mom."

"Are the crew friendly?"

"Yes, they're really nice."

I told Mom how to contact me via e-mail and she told me a little about what was going on with the media. Apparently, news people were going nuts, pointing the finger at my dad. I later found out that she didn't tell me much because she didn't want to overwhelm me.

"Do you have any idea where they're taking you?" she asked.

"No, I have no idea."

Some of the crew had tried to tell me, "Kerguelen Island," and of course I knew exactly where that was. But the way they were saying it—*Isle de Something*—I couldn't understand it. Later, though, Captain LeMoigne, who did speak a little English, pointed out our destination on a marine chart.

The captain, first mate, and one other crew member who was often up on the bridge all spoke a little English, and I really enjoyed chatting with them now and then. We talked about the work they were doing on *La Reunion*. They were fishing for what they called Tooth Fish—not the kind I saw as a kid in Mexico, but the kind known in America as Chilean sea bass.

It took us about three days to reach Kerguelen. One evening on the bridge, Captain LeMoigne and I were talking about *Wild Eyes*. I was feeling really down about having left my boat behind.

"I miss her," I told the captain.

He looked at me with the kindest eyes and said, "The boat, she can be replaced. You cannot."

 For a day or so, the world rejoiced with the Sunderlands that their daughter was safe.

After Laurence found Abby was coming home, he was happy to step outside and share his joy with reporters. One of them, from the *New York Post*, was extremely kind while interviewing Laurence in his front yard. But the next day, when her story was published, he wished he would've doused her with the garden hose.

ABBY SUNDERLAND'S DAD HAD TV DEAL AS DAUGHTER RISKED LIFE AT SEA

HERE'S A DOSE OF REALITY.

THE FATHER OF TEEN SAILOR ABBY SUNDERLAND TOLD THE POST YESTERDAY THAT HE'S BROKE AND HAD SIGNED A CONTRACT TO DO A REALITY SHOW, "ADVENTURES IN SUNDERLAND," ABOUT HIS FAMILY OF DAREDEVIL KIDS WEEKS AFTER SHE SET OFF ON HER DOOMED AND DANGEROUS SOLO SAIL AROUND THE GLOBE.

LAURENCE SUNDERLAND, A SAILING INSTRUCTOR WHO LIVES IN THE MIDDLE-CLASS LOS ANGELES SUBURB OF THOUSAND OAKS WITH HIS PREGNANT WIFE AND SEVEN KIDS, OPENED THEIR HOME TO FILM CREWS FOUR MONTHS AGO.

"THE SHOW MIGHT BE ABOUT FAMILY, IT MIGHT BE
ABOUT ABIGAIL'S TRIP. IT'S SOMETHING THAT WAS
SHOPPED AROUND," HE SAID . . . [1]

Among many American journalists and commentators, there is an article of faith: Someone Must Be Blamed.

The *Post*'s reality show "revelation" became the pulpit from which many media preached. The Sunderlands were exploiting their children, some commentators said, by presenting them as daredevil role models in a show based on their daredevil kids. Dr. Laura Schlessinger criticized the Sunderlands; others said the Sunderland parents should be thrown in jail.

CHAPTER 16

HOMECOMING

THOUSAND OAKS, CALIFORNIA
JUNE–JULY 2010

 It was nighttime when *La Reunion* reached Kerguelen. I said my goodbyes and thank you's to Captain LeMoigne and his crew. Then I rode a dinghy to the freighter *Osirus*, which took me to Reunion Island, where I met Zac, Bill, Jeff, and a man named Lyall Mercer, who had come alongside our family to help with PR.

The trip to Reunion Island took ten days. The crew spoke very little English, but between what they did speak and improvised sign language we managed to communicate pretty well. The crew was so kind to me, and every night the captain personally came to get me to make sure I ate my dinner. On June 25 when we landed at Reunion Island, it felt a little strange saying goodbye to these wonderful people who had played such a special part in my life, knowing that I would probably never see them again.

It also felt a little strange being really happy to see Zac, who had spent my whole trip making faces at me over Skype. But it was so great to see him. So great to fall into the arms of family. He brought some clothes onto *Osirus* so I wouldn't have to meet the press in oversize men's shorts and a bathing suit top. When I walked down the gangplank, we found several reporters and a whole crowd of well-wishers. We could barely push our way through all the people. As soon as I hit dry land, I gave a little press conference. I hadn't spoken such a long stream of English in so long that I surprised myself when I didn't want to stop.

Getting home was a major marathon. We flew from Reunion Island through Paris (where Zac and I had just enough time to get our photos snapped in front of the Eiffel Tower), then on to Los Angeles. I was home—back in sunny, warm Southern California, and I wasn't sure what to expect.

At baggage claim, a group of policemen talked with Lyall and Jeff, discussing the best way to get me out of the airport without having to wind through the crowd of reporters we had learned were waiting for me just outside our gate. I had had enough of being in the spotlight. Even with my team there, I didn't want to do the media thing again.

Our baggage in hand, the police escorted us down a hall to a rear exit where cars were waiting for us. Leaving LAX, we drove behind many cameramen and reporters whose backs were to the street. I felt a little bad as I wondered how long they would stand there waiting for me. But I also laughed a little with relief. At that point, my mind was on complete overload. I needed some time to sort out my own thoughts before people started asking me what they were.

There were two cars, one with Bill and Vivian, a producer with NBC; I was riding with Jeff, Zac, and Lyall. Since Vivian was going to film me going into my house, the other car drove ahead and we decided to go down to the marina to give them a little time to get to our house first.

I hopped out of the car in Marina del Rey and looked across the water. It was perfectly still and reflected the moonlight like a mirror. I walked along the fence in the silence of the night. The scene was so peaceful, and I wasn't sure I was ready to go home. But tonight that wasn't my choice. The time had come to face the fact that my life was right back where I started.

Or least, that's what I thought at the time. After a quiet ride home, we turned the corner to my house and I saw that life had definitely changed. This was my quiet little street where nothing much ever happened. Now it looked like a carnival! Vans, satellite trucks, bright lights, and a crowd of reporters milling around with cameras and mics. The sight hit me hard.

We pulled up into the driveway, and the swarm of reporters and cameras crammed in behind us. Lyall got out of the car and I followed. Then I stopped, turned, and looked back toward the street in amazement. Camera flashes fired crazily, people yelled over each other asking questions, fighting to get close enough to jam their mics in my face.

"Abby, how does it feel to be home?"

"Are you disappointed you didn't make it?"

"Abby, over here! Over here!"

Jeff stepped out of the car behind me, between the reporters and me, and I turned to follow Lyall into the house.

My house.

I will never forget the feeling of walking into my home, a place that while drifting helpless in the middle of the Indian Ocean, I wondered if I would ever see again.

As soon as I set foot in the family room, my world exploded into a blur of hugs. Dad folded me into his arms with tears in his eyes. Mom got as close as she could to hug me (she was *a lot* more pregnant than when I'd left Marina del Rey and due to deliver the very next day). Jessica and Toby jumped up and down to get my attention. My little sister Katherine hadn't been told about my accident and rescue because she was too young to understand. But it seemed she knew something had been badly wrong because she now jumped up in my arms and refused to get down. Three-year-old Ben pulled at my knees, crying to be held, too.

 Mom and Dad thought it would be a good idea if I had a little downtime before meeting the press again. But we ended up giving a press conference at the Del Rey Hotel the very next day.

I had come full circle. Not the *whole* circle, and not the way I wanted. But I knew my trip hadn't ended because of my boat or my training. And I definitely knew that rogue waves don't care how old a sailor is. So when I began taking questions from reporters, I felt confident.

"I'm really happy to be home, very sad things didn't work out," I told reporters. "I have sailed twelve thousand miles and I am proud of my achievement. The more I sail, the more I like sailing."

I knew my parents had been under attack and I defended them.

Jeff Casher had tried to defend my parents on *Geraldo*, I found out. Geraldo Rivera aired an "exclusive" in which Ted Caloroso made a bunch of false claims: that my dad pushed me into the solo-round so he could get rich off a reality show. That I was rushed out to meet a sponsor deadline. That my dad was a "stage father" who dreamed up the whole trip so I could go for this record.

Geraldo also brought on a guest named Dr. Derrick Fries and introduced him as "probably one of the foremost sailing experts on the planet." Dr. Fries *is* an expert sailor, but of Sunfish- and Sailfish-type boats, which are like surfboards with sails that you race around a harbor. Dr. Fries didn't have a lot of open ocean sailing experience, but Geraldo brought him on the show as his "expert" commentator on my sail.

Geraldo said that Captain LeMoigne, who had helped rescue me, "almost drowned." That's not true. I was there.

Geraldo said I was lucky my mast didn't puncture my hull and sink me. Wrong. My hull was punctured, but the watertight bulkheads worked to isolate the flooding and *Wild Eyes* stayed afloat—just as Dad had known she would.

Geraldo said I was sailing five hundred miles north of Antarctica. Maybe an error, maybe hype. Kerguelen Island is technically part of Antarctica, but I was actually more than 1,800 miles from the Antarctic continent.

Geraldo also brought on as a guest Jeff Casher, who actually *is* an open-ocean sailing expert. But Geraldo never mentioned that. Instead, he started rattling off questions as though Geraldo was a prosecutor and Jeff was the accused.

"It was winter, it is the height of irresponsibility to allow a child, indeed almost any sailor in a vessel of that size to sail in those waters," Geraldo said.

"Well, I think there's a lot of disagreement," Jeff answered. "You'll probably find people on both sides of that argument—"

Geraldo cut him off. Jeff later said he probably would've been treated more fairly on the *Jerry Springer* show. At least there, you get to talk.

Back at the Del Rey Hotel press conference, I was surprised that people were still freaked out about my age.

"I've sailed around Cape Horn and Cape Agulhas," I said. "The question over my age should have been over weeks ago."

I was having fun talking about my trip, and I especially enjoyed it when Lyall announced that my mom was in labor at that very moment, and that by the end of the press conference I would probably have a new baby brother. We had already decided to name him Paul-Louis, after Paul-Louis LeMoigne, the French fishing boat captain who had saved my life.

The reporters were asking good questions and they seemed to appreciate my answers. I could've talked on and on. That really surprised me.

What? Me? Talk on and on? To reporters?

In my old, "normal" life at home, I had been afraid of so many things. Of people. Of making mistakes. Of embarrassing myself. I had seen myself as this sort of shy, quiet homeschooler who preferred to be alone rather than with groups of friends. But my trip broke me out into a whole new world—filmmakers, fishermen, pilots, teachers, technicians, mechanics, scientists, little kids. Americans, Mexicans, Argentines, South Africans, Australians, and Frenchmen. So many people cared and helped and cheered me on, shaping and changing my life forever.

I am not the same person who set sail from Marina del Rey on January 23, 2010. After being bashed around in stormy seas, hand steering through freezing rain, rebuilding autopilots, rounding Cape Horn, and surviving the Southern Ocean, I have a lot different take on life than before. Alone with myself at sea for months, I learned who I am. I made some mistakes, but survived them and learned. I am twelve thousand miles wiser, twelve thousand miles more resilient, and I have twelve thousand miles more faith in God.

I have also learned that not succeeding isn't necessarily the same thing as failure. So many cool things have happened because my trip ended the way it did. Four months after my return, I was a little shocked to find myself at NASA in Washington, DC, giving a presentation to a group of congressional staffers. The NASA search-and-rescue mission team had proposed a second-generation satellite beacon system and was seeking congressional funding for it. An important part of the funding process was bringing congressional staffers to NASA, briefing them on how the system works, and showing how it will benefit people.

Strangely, my "failure" was NASA's success. It felt funny—me, just a sixteen-year-old girl standing in front of all these important people with nothing but my story. But I was a voice for all those who have had to be rescued, who would need to be rescued, and sadly, for those who had not been rescued. I was living proof that the current system works.

I was also able to provide insight into what might help the next system work even better, like enabling direct communication links between the lost and area rescue centers like the one at Canberra.

Besides speaking at NASA, I've visited the Naval Academy at Annapolis (where they wanted to recruit me for the sailing team!) and spoken at the National Oceanic and Atmospheric Administration, the University of Maryland, and several yacht clubs around the country.

Wherever I share my story, it seems to hold extra weight, partly because I had been stranded in one of the most isolated places on the planet, and partly because of my age. Most people give me credit for having sailed *Wild Eyes* around Cape Horn, then halfway around the world. But there are still some who think I was doomed to fail from the start; that I only made it as far as I did because of dumb luck. I have for quite some time now accepted the fact that I will never be able to please everyone.

I know there's been a lot of debate about the price of rescues. Critics have said it's not fair that the people and their tax money had to pay for mine. But I also know that the American people would gladly do for anyone from any country the very same thing that I'm so grateful the Australian and French people did for me.

I will definitely attempt to sail around the world again. In fact, I can't wait for the chance to try again. I might succeed and I might not. A lot of times the things that are most worth doing involve risk, and I'm living proof that not everything works out the way you planned. But I have learned an important truth: In stepping out and trying to achieve great things, the only way I can truly fail is never to try at all.

THE END

NOTES

Chapter 1

1. Scott Jutson, "Designer recounts Wild Eyes' intent," *Soundings*, August 2010.

Chapter 6

1. *Sailing Anarchy*, January 24, 2010, http://forums.sailinganarchy.com/index.php?showtopic=102689 (accessed January 21, 2011).
2. Ibid., January 25, 2010 (accessed January 21, 2011).

Chapter 7

1. Kevin Modesti, *Los Angeles Daily News*, January 25, 2010, http://www.dailynews.com/news/ci_14257254 (accessed January 21, 2011).

Chapter 9

1. *Sailing Anarchy*, February 1, 2010 (accessed January 21, 2011).

Chapter 10

1. *Sailing Anarchy*, June 16, 2010, http://www.sailinganarchy.com/article.php?get=5761 (accessed January 21, 2011).

Chapter 15

1. Anita Bennett in Thousand Oaks, Calif., and Annie Karni in New York, *New York Post*, June 14, 2010, http://www.nypost.com/p/news/national/sail_kid_parents_set_cour_for_tv_crGRuKCVBcBCM5v-3s23ULK (accessed January 21, 2011).

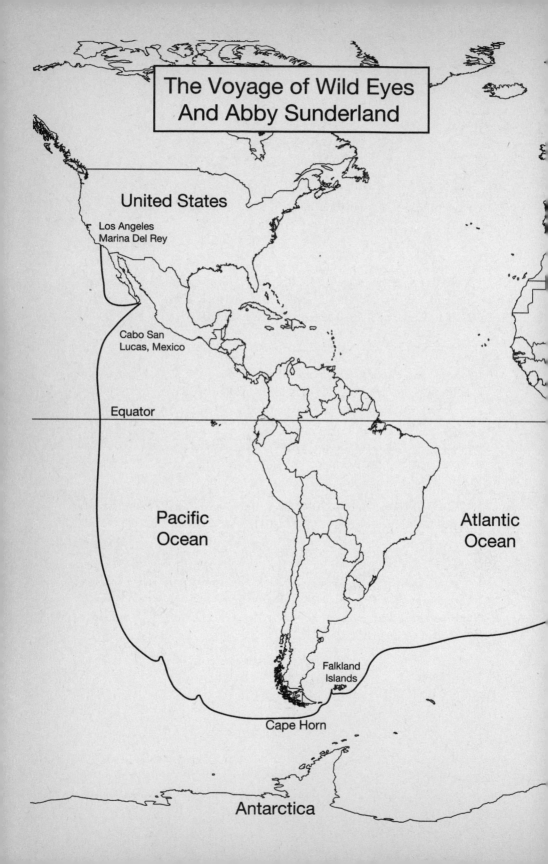

The Voyage of Wild Eyes
And Abby Sunderland

United States

Los Angeles
Marina Del Rey

Cabo San
Lucas, Mexico

Equator

**Pacific
Ocean**

**Atlantic
Ocean**

Falkland
Islands

Cape Horn

Antarctica

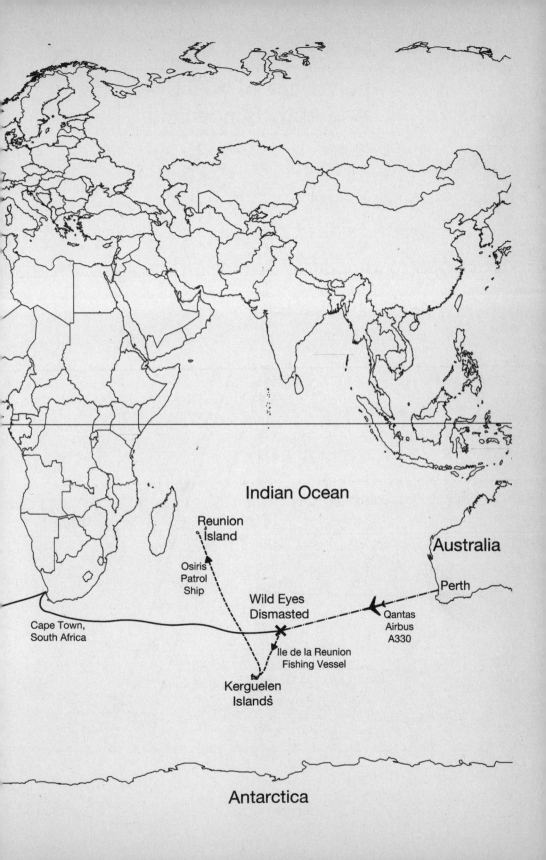

Indian Ocean

Reunion
Island

Osiris
Patrol
Ship

Australia

Perth

Wild Eyes
Dismasted

Cape Town,
South Africa

Qantas
Airbus
A330

Ile de la Reunion
Fishing Vessel

Kerguelen
Islands

Antarctica

Wild Eyes

Abby Sunderland's Open 40 Sailboat

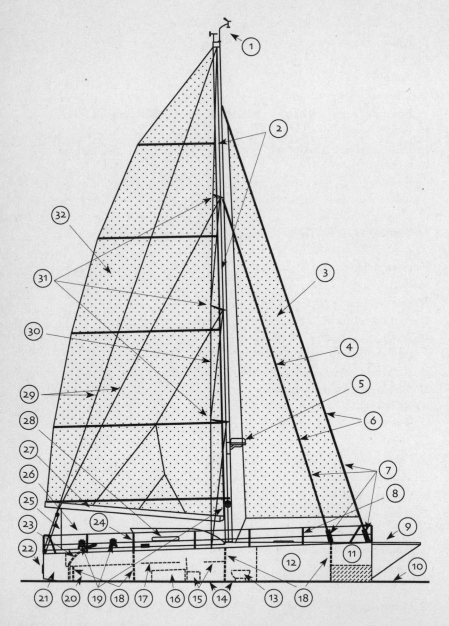

KEY

1. Wind Sensing Instruments
2. Mast: Carbon Fiber, 65 feet (19.8m) tall
3. Jib, Genoa, or "Genny," shown unfurled or "out"
4. Stay Sail, shown furled or "rolled up" around inner stay
5. Radar antenna, mounted in a gimbal which is bolted to the mast
6. Stays, fore and inner
7. Roller furling
8. Life lines (safety railing)
9. Bowsprit, secures the bottom of the spinnaker or code zero sails
10. Waterline
11. Bow compartment, half full of flotation foam, enclosed by crash bulkhead, watertight
12. Forward sail compartment: sails, food, clothing, anchors, spare tiller and rudder
13. Head (toilet) and shower
14. Hull: epoxy-glass foam, sheathed with Kevlar inside and out, 40 feet (12m) long, 11 feet (3.3m) wide
15. Chart desk and seat
16. Engine cover box
17. Bunk on port side, galley (kitchen) on starboard side
18. Four watertight bulkheads, with watertight hatches
19. Winches: six, four on the sides of the cockpit, two on either side of the mast, hand cranked
20. Aft compartment, fuel and water tanks, storage, tools, and spare parts
21. Aft watertight steering compartment, where the dual autopilot drive systems are located
22. Rear escape hatch, watertight
23. Tiller, used for hand steering
24. Cabin companionway hatch, watertight
25. Main sail sheet
26. Cockpit, open
27. Boom
28. Cabin, enclosed, 10 feet by 8 feet (3m x 2.4m)
29. Running back stays, one set on each side
30. Shrouds, both sides
31. Spreaders, three per side
32. Main sail, shown fully "up," can be reduced in area by "reefing" in three steps

BRIEF GUIDE TO BASIC NAUTICAL TERMS

aft. The back end of the boat.

anchor. A device used to prevent or slow the motion of a boat. It is deployed off the boat (usually from the bow or stern) and attached to the boat with a line. Usually an anchor is in reference to a metal wedge-type device that is designed to dig into the sea floor and then hold a boat in place. There are many different anchor designs that are relatively effective. The term *anchor* can also be in reference to a sea anchor, which is essentially a small parachute that is deployed under water. A sea anchor is designed to slow a boat in heavy seas, and keep the boat pointed in a specific direction relative to wave action.

autopilot. An autopilot is a mechanical, electrical, or hydraulic system used to guide a boat without assistance from a human being.

backstay. A backstay is the stay that runs from the top of the mast to the stern of the boat. Like other stays, it is a strong wire, rod, or line that is used to prevent the mast from being blown over. The backstay is specifically designed to prevent the mast from blowing forward.

ballast tank. Two tanks on either side of the boat. They are to counteract the heel of the boat by filling the tank on the high side, which helps to increase speed.

boom. A boom is a horizontal spar that is generally attached to the mast at one end, and attached to the aft corner of a sail (the clew) at the other end. The boom is used to hold the sail out in a horizontal direction.

bow. The bow is a nautical term used to describe the front of the boat.

bowsprit. The bowsprit is a spar that extends forward of the hull of a boat. It can be used for a variety of things, including a more forward point to attach a forestay and/or a sail such as a spinnaker or jib. (In *Wild Eyes'* case it was used to fly the Code Zero.)

bulkhead. The interior of the hull, essentially the "walls" inside the boat.

cabin. The cabin of a boat is essentially the interior living space of a boat.

close hauled. A boat is sailing close hauled when its sails are trimmed in tightly and it is sailing as close to the wind as it can without entering in irons. This point of sail lets the boat travel diagonally upwind.

Code Zero. A light sail used a lot on the equator or whenever in lighter winds. Somewhat like a spinnaker, but easier to use when single-handing.

companionway. The companionway is the entrance to the cabin of a boat. Typically there is a form of ladder or steep steps that leads from the companionway opening on deck down into the cabin of a sailboat.

deck. The deck of a boat is the horizontal outside surface that one walks upon.

down wind. On this point of sail, the wind is coming from directly behind the boat. Because running is the most difficult point of sail for modern yachts, and can be dangerous to those on board in the event of an accidental jibe.

draft. The vertical distance, or depth, measured from the waterline to the lowest point of the boat.

forestay. A piece of standing rigging that keeps the mast from falling backward, one end is attached to the top of the mast, the other to the bow of the boat. Sometimes referred to as the "stay."

furl. To take a sail, or sails, down. Furling can be done by simply lowering a sail or by rolling it using a furling device.

genoa, "jib," "genny." The larger and closer to the front of the two headsails.

halyard. Any line that is used to haul things up and down a mast. Its most common function is to raise and lower sails.

hatch. An opening in the deck of a boat that can be tightly closed or sealed if necessary to prevent water from entering the cabin.

head. The bathroom on a boat.

heel. The angle at which a boat leans over when sailing.

heaving to. Putting the boat into the wind and balancing the sails so that the boat is stationary and does not need to be helmed.

hull. The main structural outer skin of a boat. Most modern boats have fiberglass hulls.

jack lines. The lines running up either side of the boat that Abby would clip onto before leaving the cabin of the boat.

jibe. Turning the stern of the boat through the wind with the sails changing the side they fill on.

keel. The part of a boat's hull that extends below the waterline, on the boat's centerline, that is used to counterbalance the tendency of wind to blow a sailboat over. It also will always have weight at its lowest point to prevent the sailboat from tipping over.

knot. Slang for "nautical mile per hour." The standard measuring unit for speed on a boat. One knot is equal to 1.15 miles per hour. Both boat speed and wind speed are measured in knots.

lazy jacks. To assist in sail handling during reefing and furling. They consist of a network of cordage that is rigged to a point on the mast and to a series of points on either side of the boom; these lines form a cradle that helps to guide the sail onto the boom when it is lowered, reducing the crew needed to secure the sail.

leeward. A reference to the downwind side of a thing that the wind is blowing toward. Often the term *leeward* is used to describe the position of something relative to a boat.

mainsail. The sail that is located aft of the mast on a sloop.

mainsheet. The line that is used to control how far out the mainsail goes. The mainsheet attaches to the end of the boom and comes back to the cockpit for control by the crew.

mast. The vertical spars on boats. A mast is supported by stays so that it does not blow over from the force of the sails. The purpose of the mast is to provide the basic support for the system of sails.

port. The left side of something, or the direction "left."

radar. An object detection system that uses electromagnetic waves, specifically radio waves, to identify the range, direction, and speed of other boats.

reefing. A system to let down and secure portions of a sail in heavy wind. *Wild Eyes* had three reefs in her main, often referred to as the 1st, 2nd, and 3rd reef.

rig. All of the superstructure on a sailboat used to support the sails. The rig mainly includes the mast, spreaders, and stays.

roller furler. A method of furling or reefing a sail where the sail is rolled around a forestay (stay).

running rigging. The running rigging of a sailing vessel is used for raising, lowering, and controlling the sails.

sheet. The lines run back to the cockpit on either side of the boat, used to pull the jib and staysail out.

shroud. The sidestays that prevent sideways motion of the mast. Often multiple sets of shrouds will be used on each side of the mast. The shrouds will each go to different heights on the mast, as opposed to only going to the top of the mast. This is to prevent bowing of the mast under load from the sails.

sloop. A sailboat with only one mast.

spar. Any rigid pole used to help support the sails on a sailboat. Typical spars include masts, booms, spinnaker poles, and bowsprits.

spinnaker. A large sail flown from the bow of a boat that is only connected to the boat at the sail's three corners (the clew, tack, and head). Spinnakers are generally used for downwind sailing and can be difficult to control.

spreader. Spars on a sailboat mast used to deflect the shrouds to allow them to better support the mast. *Wild Eyes* had three sets of spreaders.

stanchion. The vertical supports for the "railing" around the edge of a boat.

standing rigging. The rigging components of a sailing vessel that are fixed in position while a boat is under sail, such as the lines, wires, or rods that hold up the mast.

starboard. The right side of something, or the direction "right."

stay. A wire, rod, or line used to hold a mast in place. In general a sailboat has a forestay (coming from the bow to the masthead), sidestays (coming from the side of the boat), and a backstay (coming from the stern of the boat to the masthead). *Wild Eyes* had two sets of backstays.

staysail. Second foresail, small and stronger for use in heavier winds.

stern. The back of a boat.

tack. Turning the bow of the boat through the wind with the sails changing the side they fill on.

winch. A drum-type device used to pull lines in when a significant amount of force is on the line. Winches allow the operator to use a mechanical advantage to bring in a sail.

wind generators. A system that uses the wind to generate power.

windward. A reference to the upwind side of a thing. Often the term *windward* is used to describe the position of something relative to a boat.

ACKNOWLEDGMENTS

Through my trip I have met some of the most amazing people. So many people have come on board to help me take a shot at my dream. My trip was classified as solo, but that's not entirely true. Yes, I was the only person on *Wild Eyes*, but I had such a great support crew. Yes, when it came right down to it, it was me and the water and it was me that had to make the final decisions, but without my team I wouldn't have been able to even get to the starting line.

My team was one of the best ever, and the greatest thing about them is that even back on land they're still my team; they're all there to help me out in everything from getting the toaster to work, to teaching me how to drive . . . I love you guys, you're the best!

Thank you to the Australian Maritime Safety Authority's Rescue Coordination Center, Maritime RCC La Reunion, Western Australian

Police, Fire and Emergency Services Authority of Western Australia, and French and American search and rescue teams for all they did to save me. You all went above and beyond what any of us would have expected and did it with honor. I would not be here today if it were not for you all.

Thank you to Michael Wear from Australian Search and Rescue for agreeing to go to work on your day off and being a part of my rescue. Thank you also for taking the time to come and visit my family and me during your trip to the US.

Thank you to Peter Chisolm—US Consul for Mauritius, Reunion, and the Seychelles. Thank you for helping to coordinate on my behalf during my time in La Reunion.

Very big thank you to Captain Paul-Louis LeMoigne and crew of the French fishing vessel, *Ile de la Reunion* for detouring to pick me up and for all you did to get me back home safely. You guys are all great, and I'll never forget my few days aboard the *Ile de la Reunion*.

Thank you to Captain Jacques Deshayes and crew of the *Osiris* who took me from Kerguelen Island to Reunion Island. You guys did so much to help me in those rough few days and I am very grateful.

Thanks to Nathalie Deschamps and all the people of Kerguelen Island for their incredible hospitality. You guys have an awesome little island there. Maybe on my next visit I'll have enough time to go see some penguins.

Lyall Mercer, your help with the media after my trip was amazing. I don't know what we would have done without you. It was and is still great to have you on board.

Thank you to Christian Pinkston for stepping in and helping us with the media amid your father's illness and guiding us through a painful and difficult time.

Thank you to Elton Galleghly, who called the State Department, the Office of the Defense Secretary, and the U.S. Coast Guard to ensure that a coordinated search and rescue effort was underway.

To Mom and Dad: thank you for raising me to follow my dreams, for raising me to be independent, and having the confidence in me to let me make my own decisions.

To my brothers and sisters: Toby, Jessie, Lydia, Katherine, and Ben, for being patient with me and helping out so much so that Mom and Dad could help me.

Thank you to Zac for teasing me until I had to sail around the world to silence you! Thank you for coming out to La Reunion to greet me. It meant the world to me.

To Grandma: thank you for supporting me even though I know you would have preferred that I didn't go!

A huge thank you to Ken and Bryn Campbell, George and Deb Caras, and Chris Wasserback at Commanders' Weather for your diligent weather reporting and routing instructions. I couldn't have asked for a better or more experienced group of meteorologists.

Thank you to Kelly King at Villa del Mar Marina in Marina del Rey. Thank you for finding us a slip and for putting up with our beehive of activity!

Thank you to Steve Kaufman and Matt Tolnick at Kaufman Sports. You guys were a great support and much help in our early days.

To Mike Smith: thank you for letting us rope you in to another solo circumnavigation attempt. Your expertise and careful attention to detail were much appreciated.

To Scott Lurie and Jeff Casher: your help and commitment to my trip was awesome. I know there were times when we didn't agree 100 percent on everything, but you guys stuck with me and believed in me. I'm so glad to have had you both on my team. I appreciate all of the sleepless nights we spent working in the slip, and all the times you walked me through fixing my autopilots. Scott, I was thinking, in return for helping me fix my autopilots, maybe I could teach you how to ride a bike one day?

To Bill Bennett: though we have all had our times getting mad at your constantly clicking camera, having your photos has been great. Thank you for all of your help in Cabo and with my return.

To our lovely Lisa Gizara: thank you for being a faithful friend and terrific photographer. We can't remember a time when we didn't know you. You have been there through thick and thin and we love you! Thanks also to Erik for putting up with us!

Thank you, Jerry Nash, for all of your help on board *Wild Eyes*. I couldn't have done it without you and Brady both. Thanks also to Kristi for her huge support to the family back at the house.

To Pieter Kokelaar: thank you for helping out, not only with my trip but also with my brother's. You're a great sailor and *Lady K* is a great boat. Thank you for all the times you let us use her for photo shots and for taking the trip to Ensenada.

Alan Metzger: thank you for volunteering your time to not only install my water maker, but to become a water maker expert for the team. There were plenty of times I was pretty mad at that water maker as I spent hours bleeding the hoses, but in the end, having water was worth it and having your help and expertise was greatly appreciated.

Alan Blunt: it was good to have you on my team. Your advice and support with rigging and Southern Ocean sailing was much appreciated by all of us on the team. Maybe we could talk about a spare mast for my next trip around, what do you think? (Don't worry folks, I was just kidding there!)

To Rob Jordan: your lifetime of single-handing has given you a unique ability to advise and troubleshoot and you have been a huge help to both Zac and me on our journeys—thank you!

Sid Wing: though there were times when I thought you were trying to kill me with all the training, it was all for good in the end, and I thank you for pushing me to do my best.

Thank you to Dr. David Lowenberg for offering your medical advice before, during, and after my trip. Thank you for caring so much and for helping to put together a fantastic medical kit.

Kristy Morrell: thank you for volunteering to help me plan for my nutritional needs during my trip. Thank you also for coordinating with Mountain House to choose the healthiest dehydrated food.

To Wendy and Michael Goode: you guys are awesome! I loved being on the same dock as you. We're all lucky to have known you. Thanks so much for everything you did to help out with the healthy food sponsorships as I was preparing for my trip.

Thank you to Raymond Cheng for running my website so faithfully!

Thank you to Nate 'n Al's Deli in Thousand Oaks for hosting my going away party. Great food and great times!

Thank you to Sherry Barone and the Del Rey Yacht Club for hosting my departure.

To my many sponsors: thank you for believing in me and helping me to achieve my dream.

Thanks especially to Shoe City. You were an awesome support both financially and personally with your commitment to seeing my trip through to the very end.

Thanks also to Krikorian Premier Theaters, SS Aquafriends, and Lucky Kat TV.

A huge thank you to Tammy Schroeder for pulling together the Krikorian sponsorship and fighting and praying like mad to get so much equipment sponsored.

Thank you to Dr. Ch'en at Microwave Monolithics for supporting my trip and for designing the best Personal Locator Beacon out there. We hoped I wouldn't need to use it but I was so glad to have the Micro PLB when I was stranded at sea.

Thanks to UK Halsey Sailmakers for your super professional service and round-the-world support.

Thank you to Mountain House for providing such a great variety of great food. Thank you for believing in me and stepping out into new territory to support me. Your food is the best!

Thank you to Sat West for providing a phone and discounted Iridium satellite phone minutes for my trip.

Thank you to Thrane & Thrane for sponsoring the Sailor 250 FleetBroadband system that kept me in touch with the world.

Thank you to GMPCS Personal Communications for sponsoring my Inmarsat minutes.

Thank you to Panasonic for sponsoring me two Toughbook computers. They worked perfectly for the whole trip. Awesome!

Thank you to Richard Meyers and Wraps by Rich for redesigning *Wild Eyes'* eyes and other signage. Your faithfulness and support are much appreciated.

Thank you to Vesper Marine for sponsoring an AIS system that gave me so much peace of mind while I was out there.

To Bayou Marine Electronics—you guys are awesome! If it wasn't for you, I would not have had the Thrane & Thrane Sailor 250, that excellent back-up satellite system. Thank you for being the only supplier to go the extra mile to find a system for me.

Thank you to Navionics for sponsoring all of my electronic charts for around the world.

Thank you to BilgAlarm for completely revamping my bilge pump and alarm systems.

Thank you to GoPro for sponsoring three point-of-view cameras.

Thank you to Samy from Samy's Camera for providing cameras and accessories.

Thank you to my many healthy food sponsors: Organic Food Bar, Soleo Organics, Navitas Naturals, Two Moms in the Raw, Sprout Living, e3live, Essential Living Foods, FarmaSea Health, and Environ.

Thank you to the awesome people at Winch Bit who insisted on sponsoring me when I found out about their great product.

Thank you to Chris Golden, dubbed St. Christopher, for your amazing help in Cabo San Lucas.

Thank you also to IGY Marina Cabo San Lucas for accommodating *Wild Eyes* and also providing a beautiful place to stay during our time there.

Thank you to the Cape Grace Hotel in Cape Town, South Africa, for putting the team up, feeding us, and especially for the dockside cheeseburger, fries, and Coke on ice. Amazing!

Thank you to Jeff Ayliffe, sports photographer, for being a huge part of my Cape Town stop and taking a stand in support of my trip even when others in your field didn't.

Thank you to Jannie and Tracy van Wyck for your tireless support for the team during our Cape Town stop. Thank you for making us feel like family as well as all your help with shipping odd and unusually shaped parts!

Thank you to Erik Bjerring and everyone at Wiltel Marine in Cape Town, South Africa. You were all an invaluable support to both my trip and Zac's. Thank you for finding a spot for us in the V & A Marina and basically being command central. Hope to share an African *braai* with you all soon!

Thank you to Bert Rudman, Marc Dorian, and Vivian Kim for your faithful support and accurate reporting of my trip.

Thank you to the terrific team from the *Los Angeles Times*: Pete Thomas, Al Seib, and Sachi Cunningham.

Thank you to Trond Hjerto for being a good friend and helping us out in Rhode Island.

Thank you to Dawn Riley for taking me seriously and for your advice on food, skin care, and how to keep warm.

To Stephen Mann: thank you for taking the time to talk to me and to come and check out our work on *Wild Eyes*. Your advice on the Southern Ocean was invaluable.

To Pastor Joe and Lisa Schimmel: thank you for remembering to pray for me and my family and for being there during the hours when my family did not know if I was okay.

To the many prayerful people worldwide who prayed for my safety.

To my faithful bloggers for your honest questions and (often) helpful advice. You cheered me up when I felt alone.

Thank you to Ken Wales for coming to our rescue when things looked their most bleak.

To Rick Christian, Andrea Heineke, and everyone else over at Alive Communications for believing in us and helping to make this book a reality.

Lastly, a HUGE thank you to Lynn Vincent for being open to write our story and to being faithful through trials and illness to get the job done. Thank you for being a humble conduit for our words. You rock!

ABOUT THE AUTHORS

Abby Sunderland is among the third generation in a family of sailors and adventurers. In 2007, at age 13, Abby discovered her dream of sailing solo around the world and was inspired by her brother Zac's successful circumnavigation in 2009. Her own journey, in 2010, ended in the Indian Ocean when a rogue wave rolled her sailboat, *Wild Eyes*. Abby now shares her story of tenacity and courage with audiences everywhere.

Lynn Vincent is the New York Times best-selling writer of *Heaven Is for Real*, *Same Kind of Different as Me*, and *Going Rogue: An American Life*. The author or coauthor of ten books, Lynn worked for eleven years as a writer and editor at the national news biweekly WORLD Magazine covering politics, culture, and current events. A U.S. Navy veteran, she teaches writing at colleges and conferences around the country. Lynn lives in San Diego, California.

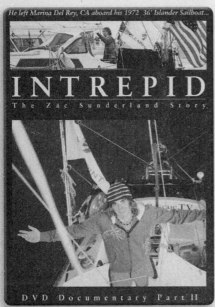
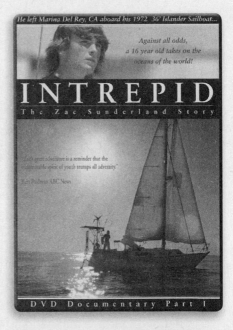